INDIAN
MOTORCYCLES

Text by Jerry Hatfield
Photography by Hans Halberstadt

MOTORBOOKS

Dedication

In memory of Ed Kretz Sr., champion of champions. He amazed us, he befriended us, he charmed us.

Acknowledgments

Thanks to the following lovers of Indian motorcycles who made this book possible: Peter Arundel, Thomas Baer, Leon Blackman, John Blackmore, Pete Bollenbach and Bollenbach Engineering, Stan Brock, Ric Brown, Max Bubek, Woody Carson, Randy Chandrasena, the late Frank Christian, Bud Cox, Billy Doyle, the late Clyde Earl, Warwick Ellis, Marvin Enochs, Bob Finn, Tom Gadd, Jeff Hackett, Dave Halliday, Gene Harper, Ray Hook, Sam Hotten, R. L. Jones, Buzz Kanter and *Indian Motorcycle Illustrated*, Tom Kowalski, Ed and Mary Kretz, Wally Krzyzanowski, Dave Leitner, Rudy Litke, Roger Long, Elmer Lower, Kay Markey, Robin Markey, Art McMullen, Don Miller, Mark Mitchell, Bill Newhouse, Marvin Niese, Dan Olberg, Herb Ottaway, Jim Parker, Dr. John Patt, Paul Pearce, Paul Pfaffle and Vintage Classics, John Rank, Larry Riedel, Jeff Roth, Bob Shingler, Pete Sink, Bob and Shorty Stary and Starklite Cycle, Jim Sutter and Indian Motorcycle Supply, Berland Sullivan, Doug Van Allen, Bob Van Farrowe, and Toney Watson.

The author is also indebted to the Research Center, Henry Ford Museum & Greenfield Village, for the use of the E. Paul du Pont Papers. All du Pont correspondence in this book is cited to "E. Paul du Pont Papers, Research Center, Henry Ford Museum & Greenfield Village."

First published in 1996 Motorbooks, an imprint of MBI Publishing Company, Galtier Plaza, Suite 200, 380 Jackson Street, St. Paul, MN 55101 USA. This edition published in 2007 by MBI Publishing Company LLC.

The information in this book is true and complete to the best of our knowledge. All recommendations are made without any guarantee on the part of the author or Publisher, who also disclaim any liability incurred in connection with the use of this data or specific details.

This publication has not been prepared, approved, or licensed by Indian Motorcycle Company.

We recognize, further, that some words, model names, and designations mentioned herein are the property of the trademark holder. We use them for identification purposes only. This is not an official publication.

Motorbooks titles are also available at discounts in bulk quantity for industrial or sales-promotional use. For details write to Special Sales Manager at MBI Publishing Company, Galtier Plaza, Suite 200, 380 Jackson Street, St. Paul, MN 55101 USA.

To find out more about our books, join us online at www.motorbooks.com.

ISBN-13: 978-0-7603-2966-5
ISBN-10: 0-7603-2966-4

Printed in China

About the Author and Photographer:
Jerry Hatfield is a longtime Indian enthusiast and the author of numerous motorcycle histories, including *Illustrated Indian Motorcycle Buyer's Guide*, *Indian Scout*, and *Indian Motorcycle Restoration Guide*.
Hans Halberstadt is a freelance writer and photographer and a fan of all things mechanical. He is the author of several titles, including *War Stories of the Green Berets* and *Battle Rattle: The Stuff a Soldier Carries*.

On the cover: The 1937 Indian Sport Four was equipped with dual Zenith carburetors, side inlet valves, overhead exhaust valves, and starburst cylinder heads. *Jeff Hackett photo, assistance by Buzz Kanter and* Indian Motorcycle Illustrated

On the frontispiece: Pointing the way to exciting miles ahead is the Indian head front fender light used on all Indian Chief models from 1947 through 1953. *Hans Halberstadt*

On the title pages: On the left, a 1920 61ci (100cc) Indian Powerplus Daytona racer built for 1-mile dirt and board track racing. On the right, a 1914 30.5ci (500cc) Indian F-head racer built for 1/2-mile dirt track racing. Restoration by Stephen Wright. *Jeff Hackett photo, assistance by Buzz Kanter and* Indian Motorcycle Illustrated

On the back cover: Sales of the 1929 Indian Scout benefited from Indian's dominance in all national championship races the previous year. However, the fact that Harley was taking a break from racing certainly helped their chances. *Hans Halberstadt*

Contents

Pedal Bikes and Motocycles

1882–1908

In 1882, 16-year-old George Hendee took his first bicycle ride on a penny farthing, one of those ancient contraptions with a giant front wheel and tiny rear wheel. With its pedals connected directly to the front wheel like a child's tricycle, it was a simple, straightforward machine. Strong legs were required to get these tall geared high-wheelers up to racing speed and then keep them there. Young George had such legs. Soon his racing exploits were thrilling crowds of 20,000 to 30,000 who packed tracks in Hartford and Buffalo, New York, and Springfield, Massachusetts. The American championships at Springfield in 1883 drew 32,000 fans from as far away as the West Coast. Seldom, if ever, had an American sporting event enjoyed such attendance. To handle the demand for these nationally publicized races, special trains were run from such distant points as Chicago. Hendee did not disappoint Springfield's huge crowd, winning the One Mile National Championship for amateurs.

1905–1909 hybrid. *The handlegrips were connected to control rods, with the left grip acting as the throttle and the right grip controlling the ignition timing. Indian was unique in using the left-hand throttle, from 1901 through 1948. The 24-hole countershaft sprocket was first pictured in 1907-model photos. This motorcycle was restored in this configuration by Henry Wing, Sr., a cofounder of the Antique Motorcycle Club of America. The machine was exhibited at the first show conducted by the club.* Jeff Hackett; assistance provided by *Indian Motorcycle Illustrated*

Though George never raced as a professional, he was matched against professionals in a number of races, and he won every time. Hendee won four more amateur One-Mile National Championships from 1883 through 1886, including a streak of three consecutive wins, which entitled him to take permanent possession of the championship medal. He also won the 2-, 5-, and 10-Mile National Championships for amateurs during this time period. Hendee entered 309 amateur contests during that four-year span, winning 302, and losing only seven! At one time or another he held all the speed records from sprints through the 50-miler.

George launched the second phase of his career upon his virtual retirement from racing in 1886. The 20-year-old Hendee tried several business ventures ultimately establishing The Hendee Manufacturing Company for the purpose of building Silver King bicycles.

In the early 1890s, personal transportation came in two types: the horse and the bicycle. There were more than 27 million horses performing all kinds of practical services, including getting from here to there when here and there weren't connected by a railroad. Unfortunately, horses, though practical in rural areas, weren't so handy in the cities where there wasn't room to quarter them either at home or at the workplace.

A new development on the bicycle front proved to be perfect urban transport. The new safety bicycle featured two equal-sized wheels and an improved gear ratio achieved by attaching the pedals and crankarms to a large sprocket amidship connected via a chain to a smaller sprocket on the rear wheel. If that sounds like the formula for today's bicycles, you're right. In the penny farthing days, the rider was perched precariously almost directly above the front axle, hence hitting a bump could launch the hapless rider over the front wheel. The safety bicycle brought the bicyclist much closer to the ground and was easier to balance because the rider sat in the middle; bumps weren't so perilous.

A few dreamers across the country were looking past the bicycle and imagining personal motorized transportation. One of these visionaries who turned the dream into reality was Springfield's J. Frank Duryea. Three years before Henry built his first Ford, Duryea was chuffing over Springfield's streets in the first successful American gasoline-powered automobile. Duryea's exploits could not have gone unnoticed by young bicycle builder and fellow citizen George Hendee. In 1895, Duryea won the *Chicago Times Herald* road race for self-propelled four-wheelers. In connection with the race, the *Times Herald* sponsored a contest to create a better name for these motor-powered devices than the current term "horseless carriage." The winning entry was "motocycle." Consciously or subconsciously, Hendee filed the name in the back of his mind.

Internal-combustion conveyances were being constructed across the Atlantic at this time as well. In 1899, a motor-powered tandem bicycle was constructed in France by Henri Fournier. The Fournier tandem was brought to New York City's Madison Square Garden to provide pacing for bicycle racing. The motor pacer's front man did the steering and the rear man took care of the engine and kept his eyes on the following bicyclist. The first rider to use the Fournier tandem for pacing found it so slow that he pulled ahead and finished on his own while the motor pacer sputtered to a noisy death before the greatly amused audience of 5,000 spectators. One of the observers was Oscar Hedstrom, a top-ranked professional bicycle racer.

His interest piqued by the pacer, Hedstrom began to study gasoline engines, and between racing dates designed and constructed his own motor-driven pacer. The Hedstrom creation, referred to by the public as an "infernal machine," debuted in December 1899 in the showroom window of the

1905–1909 hybrid. Motor number 1176 is from the 1905 range, but the valve gear is the 1906 and later style. The hacksaw-shaped pushrod dates from 1908; the mechanism actually pulls the inlet valve open. The frame and oil tank date from 1907. The tubular battery boxes on the front down tube were advertised as a new option for 1908. All 1901 through 1907 road-model Indians used battery ignition. Jeff Hackett; assistance provided by *Indian Motorcycle Illustrated*

Russel A. Frisbie store of Worcester, Massachusetts.

During this time, George Hendee had become half-owner of the Springfield Coliseum, a 1/6-mile board track or velodrome. Motor-paced racing became a popular feature in Springfield, as it had been earlier in New York.

In January 1900, Hedstrom brought his pacer to Madison Square Garden. From *Indian News* November 1940, and with the caution that Indian publicists had a knack for exaggeration, we find the following colorful account: "Its success was immediate and in the first race of the evening, it went so fast that the first racer lost pace several times and the machine had to be slowed down. Through every race, the machine ran with unfaltering success, and at the conclusion of the evening, old time racers of the 1900s were bargaining with Mr. Hedstrom to build more and more machines at any cost. A racer by the name of Dutch Waller offered him $1,000 that night for the machine—but Hedstrom did not accept. Instead, he teamed with another professional pal in the racing world, Charles S. Henshaw, scion of a wealthy family, to take on all comers. They took on all comers, too, and met with success after success. No one could defeat the team of Henshaw and Hedstrom. Before the end of the season Hedstrom built several machines and had the largest organized racing team in the world in 1900."

One of the riders Hedstrom impressed was Jake DeRosier, a man destined to become synonymous with the name "Indian."

Hendee and Hedstrom Make a Deal

Again from *Indian News* November 1940: "It was while racing at the Garden in 1900, that Mr. George M. Hendee of Springfield, Massachusetts, builder of the popular Silver King bicycle, became acquainted with Oscar Hedstrom.

"In January of 1901, on the back of an old envelope, a contract was made calling for Hedstrom to build a single-seater, motor-driven bicycle that could be produced in volume, not for pacemaking, but for the every day use of the general public."

1906. *From the 1906 catalog, "The motor bicycle . . . removes the one objection [of the pedal bicycle] that lost it so much of its favor . . . 'It's too much like work'—the objection of all save the physically gifted and the mere potterer who goes not too far, who sees little, and who dreads alike the heat, the hill, and the headwind which but add zest to motorcycling. Literally, the motorcyclist toils not while he spins; each outing is one grand, sweet, continuous coast. . ."*

On February 1, Oscar Hedstrom rented space in the bicycle plant of the Worcester Bicycle Manufacturing Company in Middletown, Connecticut. In *The Motorcyclist* September 1943, J. J. O'Conner wrote, "He brought with him his tools and his beloved pacing machines. Also, pictures of other machines he had seen at race tracks. Also some ideas and suggestions from George Hendee.

"It was typical of Oscar Hedstrom to set up a shop within a shop. He had a couple of rooms partitioned off. He arranged the work benches, installed lathes, drill presses, milling machines, a brazing outfit, grinding and buffing wheels, etc. It had everything within reason that Hedstrom

would need for experimental work. He had the only key to his shop. He specified in his deal with the plant management that he was not to have visitors and was not to be bothered with questions. He was there to do experimental work on his pacing machines, and he was to work when he pleased, day or night . . ."

On May 24, 1901, Oscar Hedstrom wired George Hendee that the Hedstrom road machine was complete. Some accounts have Oscar Hedstrom motoring confidently and dramatically over the 38 pot-holed miles from Middletown into Springfield to demonstrate his new motorcycle. However, in an interview conducted by *Indian News* for the July–August

1944 issue, Hedstrom said he shipped the first Indian to Springfield for George Hendee's approval and then came into town by train on May 30 for the demonstration on Springfield's streets.

From *Indian News* November 1940: On a day when ". . . a fellow saved his best girl and his best suit for Sundays and a promenade down Main Street, when the volunteer fire brigade was the up and coming organization of every community, when the horse drawn vehicle was the most dangerous thing on the street, when William McKinley was . . . the new 25th President of our country, when a world without war was forecasting eternal peace, everyone in Springfield let their Sunday lunch grow cold to witness the first demonstration of a motor-driven bicycle built for the public use. . ."

Hedstrom demonstrated the machine on the steep Cross Street hill, climbing the loose-gravel-surfaced, 19-percent-grade hill several times before potential investors. Following an approach speed of 25 miles per hour—fast in those days—he then throttled back to 12 miles per hour and held the same speed all the way up the 350-foot hill. Low-speed pulling power was considered important in order to woo large numbers of bicyclists to motorcycling, and Hedstrom's machine did not disappoint.

Technical Matters

The engine of the first Hedstrom model featured an overhead inlet valve contained in a removable dome. Beneath the removable cylinder head and directly below the inlet valve was the inverted, side-mounted exhaust valve. This type of engine layout has had various names. The term of a later era, "F-Head," accurately describes these engines, but at the time they were formally called inlet-over-exhaust (or I.O.E.) engines and informally called "pocket-valve" engines, the latter denoting that both valves were off the side of the cylinder bore in an imaginary pocket. (Additional confusion ensued when later literature also labeled as "pocket-valve" motors those which had both the inlet and exhaust valves on the side—more properly, these are called "side-valve" engines.) The term "F-Head" derives from the shape of the letter "F," with the stem representing the cylinder bore and the two branches the inlet and exhaust valves off to the side one above the other.

The F-Head powerplant was the standard of the day. Metallurgy was in its infancy, and there were many problems with exhaust valves melting. The principal advantage of the F-Head was the close proximity of the relatively cool inlet valve to the hotter exhaust valve: the inlet charges cooled off the exhaust valve. It was understood by theorists that this layout had the drawback of reducing volumetric efficiency because in cooling the exhaust valve the inlet charges were diluted by expansion. But at this early stage of engine development, theory was much less important than results.

1906. The 18-ci (290-cc) engine had the inlet valve on top and the exhaust valve beneath it. The single-speed machine weighed 115 pounds fully serviced and could run up to 30 miles per hour. From 1901 through 1906, oil was carried in a compartment of the fender-mounted tank. Behind the cylinder is the sight/feed oiler. A glance at this device assured the rider that oil was flowing through the engine. The exhaust cam case shown here was new for 1906 and accommodates a pivoted exhaust-valve lifter; earlier motors had the exhaust pushrod contacting the exhaust cam directly.

Oscar Hedstrom

Like George Hendee, Oscar Hedstrom had been a bicycle racer in his youth. But Hedstrom's forte was soon established as a builder of racing bicycles, rather than as a champion pedaler. Hedstrom-built racing bicycles became popular, even though some of them falsely carried the label of established bicycle companies incapable of matching Hedstrom's craftsmanship. When Hedstrom saw the need for a reliable motor-driven pacer for bicycle record setting, he built his own. The Hedstrom motor pacer was a stunning success and the impetus for the Indian motorcycle.

Through 1904, Oscar Hedstrom did some of Indian's record-setting himself. Hedstrom was a prominent figure at racing meets, where he managed the Indian team entries from 1901 to 1908. He enjoyed the financial benefits of both a high salary and royalty income from his engine and carburetor designs (Hedstrom's carburetor was a years-ahead design featuring a concentric float chamber). Meanwhile, Hedstrom expressed his mechanical engineering talents by building a seven-cylinder radial aircraft engine. The engine was used to power the first flight of airmail.

In 1913, 43-year-old Oscar Hedstrom retired from Indian, his fortune made. Hedstrom secured a country estate for his retirement in Connecticut. His engineering interest centered around speedboats, and he built champion racing boats that he piloted on the Connecticut river. In his later years his favorite pastime was hunting. Ever the craftsman, he hand carved his own gun stocks to fit his grip. He died at age 90, in 1960.

Indian cofounder Oscar Hedstrom poses proudly with a circa 1901 Indian.

1901–1902: Production Arrangements

The first Indian factory was located on the top floor of a building at 216 Worthington Street in downtown Springfield. During 1901, Oscar Hedstrom built two more motorcycles—but they weren't called motorcycles. Hendee applied the name "motocycle," the term coined after the Duryea automobile racing win of 1895. Over the years, with a rationale that escapes most enthusiasts, the Indian firm took delight in using the term "motocycle."

In 1902, Jake DeRosier went to work at the Indian factory. He gave up bicycle pacing and quickly became well-known at local race meets and hillclimbs. DeRosier left the factory after a few months to become foreman at a local garage. In July 1902, in its first public competition, Indian won the first endurance run held in the United States, a race from Boston to New York.

The Hendee Manufacturing Company continued building complete machines during 1902, but it was experiencing difficulty in achieving efficient production. Clearly, something had to be done to get the infant motorcycle company off the ground. Hendee and Hedstrom contacted several firms with the objective of subcontracting engine work. Emerging from the pack was the Aurora Automatic Machinery Company of Aurora, Illinois. On October 31, 1902, the Hendee Manufacturing Company signed a contract with Aurora by which Aurora would build the single-cylinder, Hedstrom-designed motor for Indian under the name "The Hedstrom Motor." Also, Aurora paid the Hedstrom company a royalty to build the same engine to be known as the "Thor." With the two firms now contractually bound, Oscar Hedstrom took up residence in Aurora during late 1902 and early 1903 to work out design improvements and to assist Aurora in the transition from prototypes to true production models. A total of 143 motocycles were built in 1902, but the number of Thor-built versus Indian-built engines is unknown.

1903

Indian competition successes continued in 1903. In July, at the second endurance run held in the United States, Indian won the only gold medal.

George Hendee

In 1886, after winning eight amateur high-wheel bicycle national championships, 20-year-old George Hendee quit his racing career and tried several businesses. He came up a winner with his Silver King bicycle manufacturing business, an occupation in which his racing career was an asset. Quickly, he moved into bicycle racing promotion. In 1893, Hendee crossed paths with Oscar Hedstrom, whose motor-driven pacer was in much demand at bicycle race meets because of its unprecedented reliability and performance. The pair launched a small motorcycle manufacturing business in Springfield, Massachusetts, known as The Hendee Manufacturing Company. Their machine was called the Indian motocycle.

George Hendee's organizational and political skills and Oscar Hedstrom's inventive genius proved an unbeatable combination. Together, they built the largest motorcycle manufacturing business in the world.

Hendee's business success peaked in 1913 when annual sales reached the then-astronomical figure of 32,000 motorcycles, while profit soared to $1.3 million—about $100 million in today's money. Hendee left Indian in 1916, a 50-year-old rich man. He enjoyed his retirement at a huge country estate in Connecticut.

When the United States entered WWI, George Hendee served in France as the YMCA postmaster, forwarding mail to and from 1,200 YMCA units for American servicemen. Later, he took over much of the mail responsibility for the aviation corps and ambulance service.

After the war, Hendee was instrumental in securing Springfield as the site for the northeastern states Shriners' Hospital For

Cofounder George Hendee shown aboard a 1904 Indian.

Crippled Children. George Hendee spent most of his remaining life in devotion to the hospital, where he seldom missed a day in his duties as administrator and fundraiser. He died in 1943 at 77, leaving behind his reputations as a champion athlete, a successful businessman, and a humanitarian.

The course was from New York City to Springfield and back. The Indian-mounted winner of this disputed victory was company President George Hendee. Later that year, the first American long-distance track race was won in New York City by George Holden. Holden covered 150 miles, 75 yards in the allotted 4 hours on the Brighton Beach track.

Indian faced tough competition off the track, as well. The Auto-Bi and Orient marques were launched before Indian, and their production may have rivaled or exceeded that of Indian, which produced 376 motorcycles in 1903. Of concern to Indian was the Aurora company which, in addition to its own Thor marque, was building and selling components to assemblers who then sold carbon copies of the Indian under their own labels. These assembling operations included: America, Light, Rambler, and Warwick, to which would soon be added Thor-bred and Thoroughbred. Three rival outfits were made by the giant, heavily financed Pope company: Crescent,

Imperial, and Monarch. Beyond these major players, the young motorcycle industry counted 59 other marques. And there was a newly started outfit operating out of a backyard one-room shack, but they hardly seemed a bother. The name? Harley-Davidson . . .

1904–1905

In January 1904 at Ormond Beach, Florida, Indian did a mile in 1 minute, 9-1/5 seconds, a 52-mile-per-hour pace. Another important 1904 competition win was the May 30 Fort George, New York, hillclimbing contest—not an extremely steep "bucking bronco" dirt hillclimb, but a steep uphill run over paved roads. On June 11, Indian won the 50-mile Buffalo, New York, road race in 1 hour, 11 minutes, and 30 seconds, an average of 50 miles per hour. An Indian made the 470-mile Los Angeles to San Francisco run in three days, one day quicker than the automobile record (dates not provided).

Detail improvements continued in the Indian range of single-cylinder machines, with production now up to 596 machines, an increase of nearly 60 percent over 1903. The historic "Indian Red" (then called vermilion) made its first appearance as an option to the standard Royal Blue and the optional black.

The year 1905 saw the use of a twist-grip throttle, making Indian the second marque to adopt this control (Curtiss was first). On the competition scene, DeRosier began to make his presence felt. At Cambridge, Massachusetts, he set a half-mile record of 38-4/5 seconds, a 46-mile-per-hour average. Indian's most notable result for 1905 was the climbing of the very steep Mount Washington road, a distance of eight miles navigated in 20 minutes, 59-1/5 seconds. The two-wheeler beat every automobile entered except a 60-horsepower imported car that bested the Indian by only 4/5 second. Production nearly doubled to 1,181 machines.

1906–1907

In 1906, Indian experimented with its first V-twin, which DeRosier entered in several races. The new engine was fitted to the conventional, bicycle-shaped diamond frame used by Indian since the beginning (except for one or two record-setting machines). The new twin performed well, and plans were made to add it to next year's lineup. On July 4, prominent Indian racer Stanley Kellog won the fifth annual endurance run of the Federation of American Motorcyclists (FAM), then the nation's dominant motorcycle sport sanctioning organization. In September 1906, a transcontinental record of 31-1/2 days was set by Louis J. Mueller of Cleveland and George Holden of Springfield, both Indian dealers. Annual production totaled 1,698 machines.

The headliner of the 1907 lineup was the new 39-ci (633-cc), 42-degree V-twin. The choice of a 42-degree angle—a hallmark Indian feature throughout the company's history—was based on mechanical expediency. On an engineering drawing of a single-cylinder Hedstrom motor, a line could be drawn from the center of the crankshaft to the center of the cam follower or valve lifter. If a line were then drawn from the center of the crankshaft upward along the center line of the cylinder bore, the angle between the bore center line and the cam follower center line would be 21 degrees. In order to use the same cam followers on the twins that had been used on the singles, it was necessary to offset the two cylinders by 42 degrees.

New machines prompted a need for new surroundings. Indian moved from the small Worthington Street facility to the famous "Wigwam" location at the intersection of State Street and Wilbraham Road. (The wigwam shape was not yet a fact, that would come after the premises were enlarged later.) Another benchmark occurred on March 5: the termination of the Aurora engine contract. This change was made possible by Indian's new facilities and increased manpower. At the time of the relocation there was only one building—the Mechanic Arts High School—at the State Street address. A total of 2,176 machines were built during the year, some at each facility.

Indian continued to succeed in competition, winning a prestigious 1000-mile trial in England with American T. K. Hastings at the controls. This event was the forerunner of the long-running International Six Day's Trial.

1908

During the 1908 sales season Indian was faced with growing pressure to redesign their historic line of motocycles. The bicycle-style of the 1901 through 1908 "diamond-frame" Indians made sense, technically, in this era of low power and low speed. The bicycle look also made sense in the earliest years because people were accustomed to bicycles. At first, Indian motocycle sales were largely to adult bicyclists. There were hundreds of thousands of these grown-up pedalers who were a soft touch for a machine that was a natural progression beyond the familiar pedal bike. Even the "r-less" term "motocycle" helped to set the Indian apart from challengers, to make the Indian seem friendlier and safer than rival brands. Speed wasn't important at first. Advertising emphasized endurance runs and reliability stunts, while racing took a back seat.

But racing couldn't be stopped. Racing brought bad publicity to the motorcycle movement, but good publicity to the motorcycle makers in their dog-eat-dog survival battle. Fundamentally, motorcycles weren't catching on with the mass market. The increased speeds of standard road models and increased racing emphasis had brought with them the public's apprehension about the danger of two-wheeled motoring. So motorcycling as a sport was rapidly replacing motorcycling as a practical transportation alternative.

Thus, 1908 marked the last season for mandatory, diamond-shaped (bicycle style) frames on Indians. For the 1909 season, Indian would introduce "loop-frame" models that looked like fast racers. The practical low-speed motocycle for the masses gave way to the new mainstream of the motorcycle as a sporting proposition. Indian would continue to use the r-less term "motocycle" over the coming decades, but 1908 was the last year when riding an Indian was perceived as different from riding another make. Annual production for the last all-diamond-frame lineup totaled 3,257 machines.

World Leader

1909–1915

Entering the 1909 sales season, the Indian factory, its dealers, and its riders had every right to be optimistic. But none could have guessed that in the course of the next seven years Indian would reach its all-time peak of prestige and market clout. The years 1909 through 1915 would see Indian become the world's preeminent motorcycle, proven on the race tracks of every continent, and in the showrooms of practically every nation. By 1915, Indian would be perhaps beyond challenge as the world's production leader, and certainly no American rival would ever overtake it. During those seven wonderful years of 1909 through 1915, supremacy was so clear, but, as we now know, supremacy was so temporary.

1909: Indian Joins the Styling Mainstream

In response to market demands, the 1909 Indian lineup featured new loop frames as standard issue. To eliminate old stock, diamond-frame models were continued as lower-cost options. In May, the enlargement of the new factory was underway, with Oscar Hedstrom serving as master

1915 model C-3 Big Twin with Indian sidecar. This Big Twin is a three-speed; Big Twin Models C-1 and C-2 were single- and two-speed variants. From the 1914 catalog: "The Indian Side Car offers all the pleasures of motoring for two people, in a safe, dignified and comfortable manner, at minimum cost . . . The enjoyment of motoring is made possible for the masses . . ." Owner: Jeff Roth.

architect. When completed, the works had nearly doubled in size and featured the distinctive wigwam shape, so beloved by Indian fans. A total of 4,771 machines exited the big wigwam.

Racing and other competition victories had become commonplace. Jake DeRosier affirmed his status as Indian's star rider with his achievements at the Los Angeles Coliseum board track. In October, Charles Spencer and Charles Gustafson, Jr., set amateur records from 3 to 24 hours, and for 200 through 1000 miles, at Springfield's board track. The unique, perfectly circular, 1/3-mile track was partially financed by Indian.

1910: Machine Improvements and DeRosier

The biggest functional improvements for all 1910 models were an automatic oil pump and a leaf-spring front fork. Some 1910 models also featured two-speed transmissions, footboards, starter hand cranks, and the famous Indian script. Production continued to rise and stood at 6,137 machines for 1910.

Star racer Jake DeRosier put the latest improvements to good use, twice setting 100-mile records at the Playa Del Rey mile board track in Los Angeles. He won back his 100-mile title from Morty Graves, who had briefly eclipsed him on another Indian. Running out of gas on the ninety-ninth lap, DeRosier lost about five minutes to pushing, but still beat Graves's record by almost a minute!

Apparent undercover assistance from the factory aided Fred Huyck's (pronounced "hike") setting of amateur records for 1 through 22 miles. His "amateur" times exceeded full-factory-supported DeRosier's professional times.

1911: The High-water of Indian Prestige

Indian competition prestige achieved its zenith in 1911. Amid the customary flood of racing wins, three achievements stood out: winning the Isle of Man Senior Tourist Trophy (TT), first place in The President's Race, and setting a new transcontinental record.

1915 model C-3 Big Twin with Indian sidecar. All Indians through 1915 were fitted with the Oscar Hedstrom-designed carburetor featuring a concentric, doughnut-shaped float. Unusual for the time were the removable cylinder heads, also an Indian feature since day one. The rear-stroke starter was new for 1915, along with the more substantial front chain guard. The magneto is the new-for-1915 Dixie unit.

On June 26, 1911, Volney Davis departed San Francisco on his Indian twin with the goal of establishing a new transcontinental record. This was the first of several events that would coalesce to make July 1911 the most dramatically successful month ever enjoyed by the Indian motorcycle.

On July 3, Jake DeRosier, black theatrical tights and all, lined up for the Senior TT race on the Isle of Man. At about the same time stateside, Volney Davis was arising in Salt Lake City. Forty-six minutes later, Jake, true to form, held first place in the TT, and Davis, somewhat less dramatically, was trying to find an open restaurant.

DeRosier, spilling six times during TT practice, remarked, "This ain't gonna be no picnic." The practice outing crashes left him in less than peak condition at the race's outset. After a severe crackup in the third lap while leading the race, the dazed DeRosier could manage only twelfth place. Fortunately, Indian as a team was unaffected by DeRosier's misfortune and finished one-two-three after England's own Matchless-mounted Charley Collier was disqualified from what would have otherwise been a second-place finish. The top three spots were taken by Englishman Oliver Godfrey, Irishman Charles Franklin, and Englishman A. J. Moorehouse.

The significance of Indian's Isle of Man TT sweep is still debated even among today's motoring scribes. One current historian has termed the surprisingly good performance of the English Scott two-stroke twins, including Frank Phillip's fastest lap, as the most significant development of the first TT over the long mountain course. (Previously, the TT course was a short circuit at sea level, an advantage to the popular belt-drive British motorcycles.) With this in mind, others have said that the American twins' all-chain drive and countershaft gearboxes matched against the newly laid out, steep mountain course, hastened the demise of the British belt-driven brigade.

The impact may have been even more far reaching. The famous British motorcycle journalist "Ixion" (pronounced Igs-eye-on), who wrote for *Motorcycle Illustrated* under his real name, B. H. Davies, wrote: "The trade was proposing to abandon the race next year, as it is very costly, and racing is a less remunerative advertisement with us than with you. But I do not see how it can decently be abandoned after such a smashing foreign victory."

On July 4, Erwin G. "Cannonball" Baker, later to become famous for transcontinental exploits, won The President's Race, the feature event of the Indianapolis, Indiana, July the Fourth program, which also included a staged head-on collision between two locomotives. For his victory, he was rewarded with a handshake from President William Howard Taft, the only time in American history for such an honor to come to a motorcycle racer.

Back in England on July 8, DeRosier prepared for a go at breaking his American records, using the famous Brooklands concrete oval. DeRosier's best American records were viewed skeptically by the British press. Jake put their doubts to rest, however, when he went out and equaled his best American mile effort by turning the distance in 41-1/5 seconds, 87 miles per hour. One week later, in a series of three match races, DeRosier won two races to Charley Collier's one. Collier's Matchless seemed the equal to DeRosier's Indian, but the American was too track-wise and managed to outsmart Collier in the only race not marred by equipment failure.

On July 16, Volney Davis completed his transcontinental crossing at New York City in the record time of 20 days, 9 hours, and 11 minutes. In his journey, Davis had time to sleep 4 to 6 hours every night, time to eat well, time to do an engine overhaul, time to do some mild partying, and time to stop in Cleveland to pay a respectful social call on previous record co-holder Louis Mueller. Volney Davis was the last man able to set a transcontinental record in the style of a gentleman. But don't get the idea he had an easy time of it. Repairs at a blacksmith shop, riding mile after mile over railroad cross ties, axle deep mud or sand—all were potential roadblocks to his extraordinary feat.

Indian's amazingly successful July had a rather ironic ending. Upon his return to America, Jake DeRosier was fired by George Hendee in a dispute

1913 four-horsepower, single-cylinder 30.50. *All 1913 models were fitted with the new Cradle Spring Frame, featuring swinging arm rear end suspended by leaf springs. From the 1913 catalog: "This radical new departure in motorcycle springing systems . . . marks a tremendous forward step in the quest of parlor car comfort on the highway. . ."*

1913 four-horsepower, single-cylinder 30.50. *As the name implies, this is a 30.50-ci engine. All 1901 through 1915 Indian engines were of the inlet-over-exhaust design, featuring the inlet valve on top and the exhaust valve beneath it. Both valves were offset from the cylinder bore. Magneto ignition was first offered on 1908 models as an extra-cost feature, and became standard equipment on all 1912 models. Restoration by Bollenbach Engineering.*

1913 seven-horsepower, twin-cylinder TT two-speed model. Owner Larry Riedel is justifiably proud of this original unrestored example. Acetylene lights were first cataloged on the 1905 models; electric lights weren't available until 1914.

over assignment of racing mounts. DeRosier became an Excelsior factory rider, but he never achieved the level of success he had enjoyed at Indian. At the close of 1911, Indian machines and riders held every one of the FAM's 121 recognized pro and amateur speed and distance records. Unknowingly, Indian had seen its most glorious single season.

Naturally, the vitality of the Indian company exemplified in its racing successes was equally reflected on the technical front. Extensive motor changes were made. Among the new parts were right and left flywheels, crankshaft, pinion shaft, inside (male) connecting rod, left crankcase, crankcase oil discharge, crankcase breathing valve and elbow, right and left rear motor mounting plates, front cylinder, front cylinder head for large valves, large inlet valves and valve seats, and rear cylinder head exhaust tube and union nuts. Making a last appearance on some models was the block lettering of the Indian name; all 1912 and later models until 1940 used the Indian script. Annual production for 1911 totaled 9,763 machines.

1912: TT Improvements and Racing Tragedies

In 1912, Indian Red became the standard color, displacing the previous standard of Royal Blue. Detail improvements were made to the front fork, front fender, carburetor, and cylinder heads. Taking advantage of its 1911 TT win, Indian offered TT singles and twins that featured several improvements, including knockout front and rear axles, a clutch lever moved to the right side

1913 seven-horsepower, twin-cylinder TT two-speed model. Since 1907 the Hedstrom motors had been equipped with removable inlet-valve domes. This eased maintenance because the inlet valve was removed along with the dome.

1913 seven-horsepower, twin-cylinder TT two-speed model. Hubs and spokes were nickel plated on all models from 1901 through 1914. Beginning in 1915, black hubs and spokes were phased in on some models, and by 1917 all hubs and spokes were black.

Jake DeRosier

In 1909, Jake DeRosier won every race at the March meet of the Los Angeles Coliseum board track. These wins cemented DeRosier's national status, as they were scored against California's top-billed racer Paul "Daredevil" Derkum.

In 1910, again at the Los Angeles Coliseum motordrome, DeRosier rode perhaps his most brilliant race in the United States. In attempting to lower his own 100-mile mark, Jake established new records for distances from 2 to 92 miles before running out of fuel. During this nonstop performance on his famous Number 21 F-head twin, he averaged 43-2/5 seconds per mile and covered 83 miles in the hour. DeRosier's time for 90 miles was 1 hour, 6 minutes, and 33-2/5 seconds, an average of 81 miles per hour. By comparison the fastest British 90 miles to that point was accomplished at a 49-mile-per-hour rate, and the best Continental effort was only marginally faster.

DeRosier was a member of the 1911 Indian Isle of Man TT team. He was the acknowledged prerace favorite, and caught the fancy of the British press for his self-confidence. His racing attire of black tights was a sensation. But while the Indian team finished 1-2-3, Jake finished a lowly twelfth because of several spills.

He redeemed himself the following two months, winning the much-publicized match races against English challenger Charley Collier and setting a number of records.

Racing an Excelsior in Los Angeles in March 1912, he was severely injured. In the year following, he endured three operations, finally dying on March 1, 1913.

As the DeRosier funeral procession passed the giant Indian factory, President Hendee ordered the Indian factory flag half-masted

Jake DeRosier is shown here on a 1911 racer, similar to those used that summer at the Isle of Man TT race.

and all production work halted for 5 minutes in DeRosier's honor. On the day of DeRosier's funeral, the retirement of cofounder Oscar Hedstrom became official. A hell of a day for Indian.

---

of the tank, kickstarter, footboards, larger rear hub, and double rear brake. Internally, key motor changes throughout the Indian line included new inlet-valve pushrods, inlet valves, inlet valve seats, inlet valve springs, inlet-valve-spring collars, exhaust valves, exhaust-valve springs, exhaust cams, and exhaust-cam case. Annual production totaled 19,500 machines.

Indian's record-setting ways continued in June with Charles B. Franklin setting world records for two, four, five, and six hours to become the first rider to travel 300 miles in less than 300 minutes. The venue was England's Brooklands track.

Shortly after Franklin's success, Indian, indeed U.S. motorcycle racing in general, suffered a huge setback. On September 8, 1912, on the Vail motordrome in Newark, New Jersey. Eddy Hasha's eight-valve Indian began to miss during the last race of the day, event number thirteen, and Ray Seymour shot past. Hasha reached down with his left hand to adjust something, the motorcycle at once picking up speed and closing the gap with

Seymour. In the next instant, Hasha and his Indian shot up the bank coming out of the number-four turn in front of the grandstand. By the time the machine came to rest, Hasha, a rider named Johnny Albright, and six spectators were dead or dying. The grim reality of Newark and the resulting publicity and local threats marked the beginning of a slow decline for the 1/4-mile midget motordromes, or "murderdromes," as the press referred to them. This was one of the few cases in the history of the *New York Times* that motorcycling was front page news. The Newark accident was perhaps the single most damaging blow to ever affect American motorcycling.

1913: The Cradle Spring Frame and a Notable Departure

Since its launch in 1901, Indian had offered only one major redesign, namely the loop frames brought out on the 1910 range. In 1913, another major change was made, the Cradle Spring Frame. Few American motorcycles had offered rear suspension, and none of those marques had been com-

Motordrome Action

While Indian enjoyed winning prestigious long-distance road events, much of American motorcycle racing was done on motordromes. These were short, steeply banked tracks surfaced with wood. Most of these were 1/3-mile, but some were shorter in length: a "four-lap" track was a 1/4-miler, a "six-lap" track was a 1/6-miler, and so on. The surface of these tracks was made by turning 2x4 boards on their edges, thus making the track 4 inches deep. This was necessary in order to provide sufficient rigidity to combat the stress loads of high "G" forces in the steeply banked corners. Corner banking varied from track to track, with later tracks more steeply banked than early ones, but 60 degrees became the standard.

Indian dominated motordrome racing from 1909 through 1915, partly because they had motorcycles in the hands of more riders than did rival companies. But that circumstance was partly due to Indian's early engineering lead over rival makes; most riders preferred Indian, in other words.

The peak of motordrome racing was 1912. By then, over a dozen 'dromes were scattered across the nation in such cities as Atlanta, Georgia; Chicago, Illinois; Cleveland, Ohio; Detroit, Michigan; Los Angeles, California; Newark, New Jersey; Omaha, Nebraska; and South Orange, New Jersey. Amazing speeds were run on these tiny tracks, due to the steep corner banking, and on several occasions 90-mile-per-hour averages were achieved. In retrospect, it's hardly surprising that when a major accident first occurred on a motordrome, the event was horrific. At Newark in late 1912, two riders and six spectators were killed when a rider lost control in a corner. Spectators at the motordromes had a habit

Los Angeles Stadium motordrome, 1912.

of leaning out over the track, and one onlooker was beheaded in the accident. The resulting nationwide bad publicity hastened the demise of the motordromes, most of which were closed by 1916. However, long board tracks, built primarily for auto racing, were springing up in place of the motordromes. Much motorcycle racing history remained to be written on the long boards.

---

mercially successful. Now, Indian brought out a swinging-arm rear suspension, similar in concept to modern rear-suspension systems. The Indian Cradle Spring Frame featured a pivoting rear fork moving against the pressure of twin sets of leaf springs, one set for each side of the machine. As part of the redesign, the rear part of the top frame tube had more downward slope, in order to lower the saddle height.

All 1913 Indians featured this new frame layout. This in conjunction with painting all machines Indian Red greatly simplified manufacturing management. In addition to the new frame, the tank was now narrower at the rear, and the new Superba Mesinger saddle featured leaf-spring suspension.

Oscar Hedstrom, the engineering brain behind the new frame and numerous other Indian advances, retired March 1, 1913. Hedstrom's retirement was a serious blow to future Indian progress on the tracks and in the showrooms. Mitigating the departure, the annual production of 32,000 motorcycles was an all-time high, as was the year's profit of $1.3 million.

The significance of Indian's updates and growing production would pale when compared to two other transportation events occurring in 1913. Henry Ford's first moving assembly line, and the first use of installment credit to purchase automobiles both occurred that year. As a result, passenger-car sales were up nearly 30 percent for the year, while total motorcycle sales leveled off. With low-priced cars on the horizon, the death sentence for most American motorcycle manufacturers had been issued.

1914: Motorcycling's First Electric Starter

For the 1914 lineup, Indian overstepped themselves with the Hendee Special. This was a big twin equipped with motorcycling's first electric starter. However, there was no generator, the idea being that the rider was to plan ahead and keep one of the machine's two batteries freshly charged. A further handicap to the Hendee Special was that batteries of the era weren't very reliable. This was particularly true for motorcycles because of

1914 seven-horsepower, two-speed regular model. *Among improvements for 1914 were the tank-mounted toolbox shown here, and on the "Standard" models, electric lights were provided for the first time. The two-speed transmission was introduced on some 1911 models. Owner: Tom Kowalski.*

the stress generally imposed by speed-prone riders traversing the era's rough roads. The Hendee Special lasted but one season in the United States; a few were perhaps left over for the 1915 British season because Indian stockpiled large numbers of machines in London. Other 1914 innovations included electric lights on all standard models, heavier inlet-valve rocker arms, and heavier valve domes (enclosures).

Meanwhile, at the Wigwam, an interesting development was coming to fruition in the engineering department. Whether under the influence of Indian's transatlantic contact, Charles Franklin, or worked out independently by some combination of engineering-staff talents, the Indian F-Head racing singles were being equipped with radically different cylinder heads. The combustion-chamber roof now sloped steeply toward the valve chamber, thus predating by five years the so-called squish principle designs of Britain's Sir Harry Ricardo. That Indian development arrived at the same

conclusions as Ricardo should come as no great surprise, for Indian was then the world's largest selling motorcycle, and the company possessed immense engineering capabilities. Combustion-chamber experiments at Indian in 1913 and 1914 were setting the stage for the near future when a new generation of the iron redskins would be established as the world's fastest side-valve motorcycles.

Symbolizing the nation's growing enthusiasm for motoring, the first traffic light was used in Cleveland, Ohio. Somewhat ominously, both annual production (25,000) and profit ($712,000) marked first-time-ever declines from the previous year.

Racing and record setting continued apace, with Erwin G. "Cannonball" Baker setting out May 14, 1914, on his first transcontinental record attempt. Baker used an interesting strategy. By making his departure from

continued on page 25

1915 Model C-3 Big Twin. *Indian's famous leaf-spring fork system used from 1910 through 1945. The up-and-back action was effective because it absorbed both horizontal and vertical shocks.*

Below
1914 seven-horsepower, two-speed regular model. *Big, twin-cylinder, 61-ci road models debuted in 1909; earlier road-going twins were smaller. Prior to 1910, Indians were started by pedaling bicycle style or by pushing. In 1910, some models were equipped with a removable starting hand crank applied to the end of the transmission. This forward-stroke starter was introduced on the 1912 TT models.*

1915 model C-3 Big Twin. *These were the last of the Oscar Hedstrom-designed inlet-over-exhaust or F-head models. From a 1915 sales catalog: "Its supremacy does not stop at the Atlantic and Pacific, but stretches onward to a complete encirclement of the earth."*

1915 catalog. *"Where the Indian stands for 1915. The rider has every right to expect in buying a new machine that it represents the latest motorcycle thought. As ever, the 1915 Indian lays before its friends the fullest measure of advancement . . ."*

continued from page 21

San Diego, California, during a steady rain, he was able to ride most of the distance between two weather fronts. Within an hour he was greeted by sunshine, and he didn't encounter rain again until two-thirds of the way across the continent. His record time of 11 days, 12 hours, and 10 minutes meant good-bye forever to the more civilized efforts of predecessors such as Volney Davis. Henceforth, with ever improving roads and motorcycles and with a growing population of service stations, increasing importance would be placed on the transcontinentalists' ability to go for long periods without rest or sleep. Despite somewhat better conditions than Davis encountered, Cannonball had no easy time of it. Like those who had crossed the continent before him, he had to endure axle-deep sand in the Southwest desert and axle-deep mud in the Midwest. Baker's machine was equipped with the Cradle Spring Frame, and Indian advertisements attributed much of his success to this feature.

For the July 4 holiday, the first of a series of annual 300-mile "road races" was held in the middle of the great plains in Dodge City, Kansas. Far from a genuine road race, the course consisted of a two-mile dirt oval. Glen "Slivers" Boyd, so named because of an earlier fall and resulting slide on a board track, won the 300-mile National Championship for Indian. Nobody could guess that this would be Indian's only win in the era's premier motorcycle race, and that the little backyard outfit, Harley-Davidson, would soon eclipse Indian in motorcycle racing.

1915: The New Order

Co-founder George Hendee resigned as the company's general manager in 1915. While Hendee remained as president, reports of his increasing interest in his newly constructed country estate were the evidence of a managerial chasm within the Hendee Manufacturing Company. Coupled with the 1913 departure of Oscar Hedstrom, this degradation of management expertise was to play a major role in the coming decline of Indian.

The F-Head reached its zenith in the 1915 season. This was the brainchild of the departed Oscar Hedstrom, and was complemented by the Hedstrom carburetor. The major functional changes for the 1915 F-Heads were the option of a three-speed transmission (instead of a two-speed) and the provision of a generator on all models equipped with electric lights. Signaling future economies to be applied to all models, the low-price, single-cylinder models had wheel hubs, rims, and spokes finished in Japan Black. Previously, nickel-plated hubs and spokes had been used with red rims. A new kickstarter graced all models, and it featured a rear stroke like other marques instead of the awkward forward stroke that had been unique to Indian. The ultimate Hedstrom model was the Model C-3 big twin, which featured the new three-speed transmission. With a bore and stroke of 3-1/4x3-43/64 inches, the engine displaced 60.92 ci (998.30 cc).

Despite Indian innovations, the marque no longer possessed marked technical superiority over its rivals, most of which also used the F-Head concept. Harley-Davidson was making that painfully obvious on the race tracks with their newly formed team of salaried riders backed up by a full-time racing department. Moreover, the Hedstrom motor and carburetor were expensive to manufacture. Indian was alone in using removable cylinder heads on their F-Heads, and in making its own carburetors. Indian's rivals, of which Harley-Davidson was now the strongest, got away with one-piece combined cylinders and heads and bought their carburetors from carburetor companies. Management was looking for a cheaper design to build and had found it in the form of the side-valve design. As the 1915 F-Heads appeared once again in the showrooms, the new side-valve motors were undergoing rigorous testing.

On the racing scene, Indian again found itself facing the toughest competition ever. Throughout the summer, new Indian star Ray Creviston was the dominant flat-tracker, posting wins over Excelsior's top rider Bob Perry and besting Don Johns on the sensational overhead-cam Cyclone V-twin. But Creviston's longest win was a 50-miler. Harley-Davidson countered by winning the Dodge City 300, the Saratoga (New York) 200, and the Le Grand (Oregon) 200. Excelsior's Bob Perry won the 100-mile flat track race at Madison, Wisconsin. Indian closed the heavy summer schedule by winning the 300-mile board track event at Tacoma, Washington.

Indian recovered lost prestige with the first of the so-called Three-Flag runs from Canada through California to Mexico. Cannonball Baker did the riding and managed the trip in three and a half days. Indian advertisements mysteriously referred to Baker's mount as having a new type of motor that would be standard in the forthcoming 1916 models. However, the accompanying photos showed an earlier picture of Baker on a traditional F-Head model. In fact, Baker's Three-Flag machine was one of the experimental side-valve jobs that would shortly debut in the 1916 lineup.

Production and profit continued to decline totaling 21,000 motorcycles and 3,200 sidecars and $422,000 respectively. To some extent, these statistics reflected the impact of launching an entirely new design (for 1916). Still, the situation undoubtedly looked serious to Indian management. During the year, Indian opened a Dublin depot and installed Charles Franklin as the manager.

Meanwhile, automobile production shot up dramatically. The one-year increase in car company sales dollars from 1914 to 1915, was 69 percent! Against this rise, Indian production shrunk 15 percent and profits fell by 41 percent. Harley-Davidson fared better with a 2 percent sales-dollar growth, but the era of explosive growth in the American motorcycle industry was clearly over, killed by low-priced Fords. Indian, Harley-Davidson, and the Excelsior/Henderson firms braced themselves for the coming battle to achieve larger shares of a shrinking market. Against this big-three motorcycle battle, a host of small, struggling also-rans hoped to avoid the fate of more than 80 American motorcycle manufacturers that had already gone bust.

Short-Run Profits Spell Long-Run Trouble

1916–1919

President George Hendee retired in July. His departure left Indian without the motivational spark he and Oscar Hedstrom provided as genuine motorcycle enthusiasts and pioneers. Henceforth, the company was under the complete financial control of non-enthusiasts, which set the stage for further setbacks.

When Indian closed its Dublin depot in 1916, Charles Franklin set sail for the United States, where he entered the Indian engineering department, joining Charles Gustafson, Sr., and son Charles, Jr. The Gustafsons had replaced Hedstrom's F-Head line with a side-valve design. Too late to play a major role in the Powerplus development, Franklin nevertheless soon became the driving force in development of both racing and standard machines.

In racing, board tracks were on the decline. The public's initial curiosity had been satisfied, while the dangers of the dromes had cooled the ardor of even devout motorcycle fans. Harley-Davidson never played the motordrome game and now proved that greater prestige was to be won in long

1917 Model O Light Twin. Replacing the one-year-only Featherweight was the Model O Light Twin, or as rivals called it, the Model "Nothing." No doubt the Light Twin was inspired by the transatlantic success of the British-built Douglas opposed twin, especially in that key Indian engineering department figure Charles Franklin was a recent immigrant from Ireland and had undoubtedly noticed the British bikes' success. Restoration by owner Paul Pearce.

road races. Consequently, both Indian's and Excelsior's management deemphasized motordrome racing after 1913. Some of the short dromes, such as Detroit's and Cleveland's, had quietly closed their doors after fatal accidents, and others would soon follow.

1916: The New Powerplus Range

Indian startled the motorcycle world with the 1916 Powerplus range. Gone were the famous Hedstrom motor and Hedstrom carburetor, although the latter could still be obtained by special order.

In place of the historic F-Head layout, the Powerplus line used a side-valve motor. To keep from making all Indian magnetos for twins obsolete, the 42-degree cylinder angle of the F-Head twins was continued on the Powerplus twins. The Powerplus used a slightly smaller bore and longer stroke than the F-head, its 3-1/8x3-31/32 inches yielding a displacement of 60.88 ci (997.6 cc). Like the F-Heads, the Powerplus operated all four valves from a single camshaft carrying two cam lobes. Each lobe operated both the inlet and exhaust valves of its dedicated cylinder, through pivoted bellcrank cam followers. The crankpin was beefed up, and the connecting rods were mounted on a four-row set of roller bearings. Wristpins and bearings were of larger diameter. The right (timing side) bearing was of roller design, while the left (drive) side bearing was a plain bronze bushing. As in the later Hedstrom engines, an oil line was routed to the base of the front cylinder. This was necessary to ensure adequate oil supply because the front cylinder didn't

1917 Model O Light Twin. *Described as "a radical departure" by a 1917 catalog, Indian added that the model was capable of speed from 6 to 45 miles per hour. Forecasting a vast market that included thousands of bicyclists, the catalog added, "Parents, appreciating the boon to their sons and daughters of the great body-building, eye-clearing, blood-making outdoors, will need no undue urging to persuade them to purchase . . ." In reality, the 15.7-ci side-valve twin was little more successful than the 1916 Featherweight two-stroke. The Model O was listed for the 1917, 1918, and 1919 seasons. The only significant design change during its brief career was a new leaf-spring fork for 1918.*

benefit as much as the rear cylinder from oil slinging off the crankpin, connecting rods, and flywheels. The new Powerplus side-valve twins and singles breathed through a Schebler carburetor, although the famous Hedstrom pots remained an option in order to clear stock.

Although the original motivation for the new Powerplus series was a lower-cost engine, the new motor lived up to its name and provided more punch. Indian fans were at first skeptical of these "un-Indian" motors, but were won over by the extra power, smoothness, and cleanliness of the new layout. Japan Black hubs, rims, spokes, and fittings became optional on all models.

Another new model for 1916 was the Featherweight single-cylinder two-stroke. This little 221-cc machine featured a cartridge-spring front fork like the 1906 through 1909 Indians, an outside flywheel, and a three-speed sliding-gear transmission that was a miniature version of the gearbox used on the big Indians.

The overpowering competition provided by cars caused motorcycle advertising to turn sharply away from its original technical themes. There were still mechanical details to be described, but catalog covers now established a new theme, selling the sport of motorcycling as much as the motorcycles. The motorcycle, according to the 1916 catalog cover, offered escape from the workplace and the confinements of city dwelling. A smiling Indian rider chuffed away from the office building, cheerfully waving at workmates, friends, and passersby. One man waved back while another, hands in pockets, gazed wistfully at his lucky Indian-mounted buddy, obviously on

1916 Powerplus. The 1916 Powerplus range was a dramatic departure from the Hedstrom F-head-powered predecessors. Although electric lights were available, Indian also offered acetylene lights until the mid-1920s as on this example. Owner: Tom Kowalski.

1916 catalog. "To millions of people, even though they may not ride, the word motorcycle means nothing but Indian as the word light means the sun."

the road to summer-afternoon adventure. A motorcycle was no longer mere transportation—it was a magic carpet.

1917–1919: Technical Changes

Several detail changes were made to the Powerplus series in 1917. Most visible was the new fuel/oil tank, which was more rounded and covered the top frame tube. Aluminum pistons debuted, and the toolbox was moved under the saddle. Olive drab was an optional finish. According to "Honest Injun" Article 15, a khaki finish was also optional, but this color was not mentioned in the parts books.

The little two-stroke Featherweight single, introduced the previous year, wasn't included in the 1917 lineup because of disappointing sales. However, Indian didn't give up in its attempt to market a low-cost, basic-transportation machine. The new low-bucks lightweight offering was a 257-cc horizontally opposed side-valve twin. This new Model O, derided by rival shops as the "Model Nothing," retained the general layout of the defunct two-stroke, including cartridge-spring front fork, outside flywheel, and a three-speed, sliding-gear transmission.

1916 Powerplus. *All major assemblies except the motor were left over from the F-head range. Making their last appearance were red wheel rims and nickel-plated hubs and spokes. In late 1914, Cannonball Baker rode a machine like this to set a new transcontinental record of 11 days, 12 hours, and 10 minutes.*

1916 Powerplus. *All that newly found power came from a 61-ci side-valve motor inspired by the American-made Reading-Standard motorcycle. Indian technician Charles Gustafson, Sr., had previously worked for Reading-Standard. The Powerplus motors were quieter, cleaner, and more powerful than the Hedstrom F-Head motors. As an added benefit, Indian no longer had to pay Oscar Hedstrom design royalties.*

1916 Featherweight. *Indian tried to sell this two-stroke lightweight as a low-cost, practical transportation alternative. From a 1916 catalog: "Every man's motorcycle! . . . a true lightweight motorcycle, not a motor-bicycle . . . The development of the Featherweight places at the disposal of the business and professional man, the office-worker, the factory employee, the local salesman and hundreds of other men . . . a city and suburban vehicle of remarkable convenience and service. To the parents of boys, especially, this type provides a machine that does away with all objections as to extreme power and weight . . ."*

Minor change was again the theme in 1918. The handlebars had a different shape, and cables replaced the rods, bell cranks, and telescoping tubes formerly used to actuate controls. Additionally, the handlebars were adjustable, a change permitted by the new wire controls.

The gearshift lever, shifter gate, exhaust-valve lifter, and clutch hand-operating lever were all new. The clutch hand lever also operated the external brake. The combined clutch/brake hand lever was a big improvement for riders who lived on hilly areas. When stopped on an uphill grade, the rider could resume forward progress with continuous movement of one control lever. The saddle mounting was changed so that the saddle pivoted from its new nose mounting. The belt-driven generator was separate from the magneto and was mounted low and forward of the front down tube. The new

1916 Featherweight. *The outside flywheel kept crankcase volume small, which helped the pumping action of the air/oil/fuel charge on its way through the crankcase to the cylinder. The three-speed transmission was a miniature version of the Powerplus transmission. The model was only cataloged for the 1916 season. Restoration by owner Paul Pearce.*

Cannonball Baker

Motorcycle racers in the board-track days were good at marketing themselves, and one of their favorite devices was the nickname. One of the early racers was "Slivers" Boyd, whose name came from a fall on a board track. "Speck" Warner got his name from wearing glasses (spectacles) while racing. "Fearless" Balke lived up to his name as a gutsy, give-no-quarter guy. Other nicknames were more obviously manufactured with an eye to gate receipts. "Millionaire" Morty Graves supposedly was a wealthy eccentric who raced for fun only. Yeah, sure. "Daredevil" Derkum doubtless just liked the sound of his title. It was all too much like today's professional wrestling.

Nobody lived up to their self-given name better than Erwin G. "Cannonball" Baker. He was a huge man, with hands as big as hams as one friend said. When you shook hands with him you lost your hand, said another. A handshake from "Bake," as his closest friends called him, was almost embarrassing.

Baker tried his hand at racing, but generally wasn't a winner because he was simply too large to compete against the typical tough, jockey-sized racers. But Baker discovered he had a different talent: endurance. If the grind was long enough, he could outlast anybody. Long-distance record-setting became his forte.

Erwin G. "Cannonball" Baker is seen here in Philadelphia, in 1919, while attempting another transcontinental record. Baker was later stopped by rain and mud in New Mexico, when three-fourths of the way across the continent. So he laid claim to the record for New York City to Albuquerque, a little over 3 days and 19 hours, an average of 26 miles per hour over the 2,368 miles, mostly on dirt, sand, and mud.

Baker's motorcycle world records included the following: 12-hour (track), 24-hour (track), 24-hour (road), 500-mile (track), and 1,000-mile (track). In 39 interstate endurance runs between 1909 and 1920, Cannonball made 33 perfect scores. He set road records in Tasmania, Australia, and Hawaii. The New York City to Indianapolis solo and sidecar records were his, as was the New York City to Albuquerque record. He won the 1914 El Paso to Phoenix so-called road race over 537 sandy miles. Baker was the first to make a "Three-Flag" record run, from Canada to Mexico or vice versa. Cannonball twice set the transcontinental record, in 1914 on an Indian F-head twin, and in 1922 on the Ace Four. These records are more impressive when one realizes that Baker set his records in an era when roads were treacherous at best and largely unmarked.

As a car driver, he was equally adept, setting three transcontinental records and 16 city-to-city records. By 1920, he had crossed North America 52 times by either motorcycle or car. His last motorcycle crossing was in 1941, when he tested a rotary-valve, single-cylinder model, which he had helped to design. On this run, he remarked to Indian racer Ed Kretz, "Ed, I'm not going to rust out; I'm going to wear out."

---

generator location drew criticism from dealers because of the increased likelihood of water ingestion. The tailpipe was moved to the right side.

On the Model O light twin, the front suspension was changed from a cartridge contained coil to a leaf spring for 1918. The gearshift was changed so that the small tank-top lever was rotated horizontally, which transmitted its motion through a vertical shaft. The footboards were longer and less inclined.

For 1919, a new optional finish was Indian Gray with black striping and gold borders. On Indian Red models, the trim was changed to two thin gold stripes without the broad, black inboard stripe. The left handlebar carried the lever for external brake actuation. On the right crankcase, the oil

sight glass was replaced by an oil-level plug. The Model O light twin made its last appearance this year, unrenewed due to mediocre sales.

The Impact of World War I

In early 1917, the United States entered "The Great War," as it was then known. Indian's new management saw great opportunity in the war, and contrary to long-time Indian gossip, the company did not lose money on its wartime contracts. In fact, profits for 1917, 1918, and 1919 were, respectively, $540,000; $733,000; and $937,000. The latter was the second highest annual profit in Indian history, though undoubtedly wartime

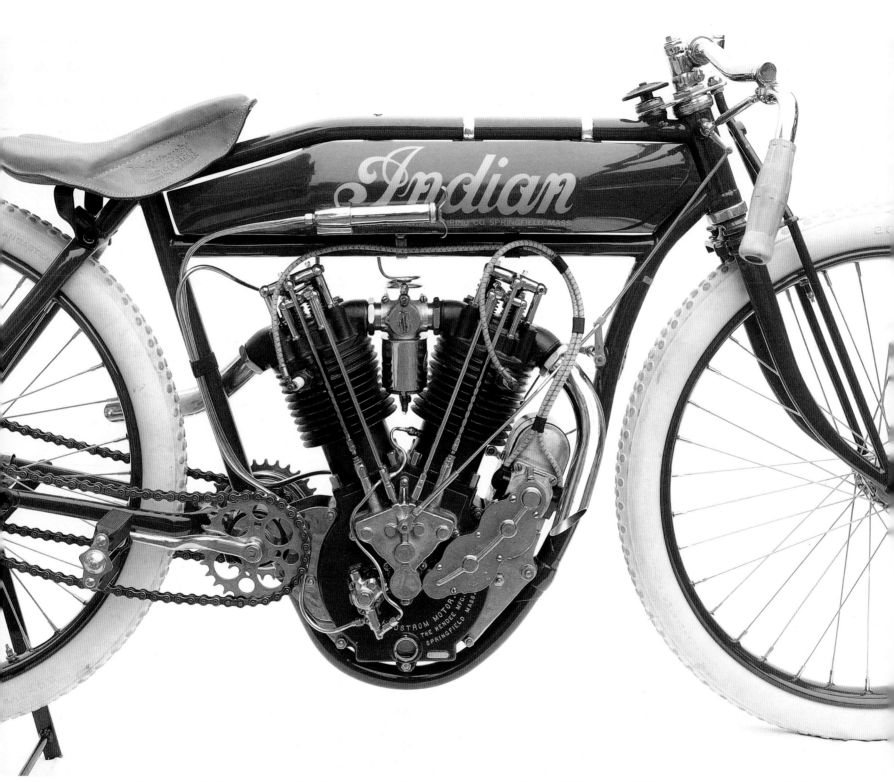

To maintain racing dominance, Indian brought out eight-overhead-valve, 61-ci racing twins in late 1911. *Around 1916, the racers were updated to the configuration shown here. The 1911–1915 "big-base" version used special large crankcases and flywheels, but the 1916 version used standard F-head cases and flywheels. The cylinders were "ported," which in this case meant slots cut in the cylinders. When the pistons moved downward they uncovered the ports and allowed rapid exhaust discharge. Due to the ports, the eight-valve twins were constantly covered with oil. Sam Hotten*

1917 Powerplus. *All crankcases were painted from 1901 through 1925. Beginning in 1926, crankcases were either painted or had a "special wire brush finish" (unpainted), according to dealer and rider preference. Few crankcases were painted from 1928 on.*

1917 Powerplus. *The Classic Cradle Spring Frame was years ahead of its time. In later years it fell into disfavor because of its appearance and the rapid wear of the swingarm bearings. Speedometer drive gears were exposed prior to the 1931 models. External, contracting-band brakes were also standard until 1931.*

1917 Powerplus. *Not completely restored, this 1917 Powerplus is missing the gold pinstriping that should be on the tanks. The new roundish tanks were not only more stylish but were cheaper to build than the earlier tanks. The 1909 through 1916 tanks had been built up by hand, by assembling several sections. The new tanks were basically stampings, although some hand assembly was still required.*

inflation diluted the value of these dollars.

However, the Army contracts did prove costly over the long haul. From *Motorcycle and Bicycle Illustrated* September 19, 1918:

"Indian Deliveries Contingent on Needs of Government—There will be Indian motorcycles, sidecars, and delivery cars for civilian buyers, but how many and when depends entirely upon the requirements of our fighting forces and those of our allies whose orders will be filled first."

Indian committed too much of its production capability to the war effort, and as a consequence, the company lost riders and dealers by not being able to supply motorcycles to the civilian market.

Production was fairly consistent during the war years, logging 20,500 in 1917, 22,000 in 1918, and 21,500 in 1919. Sidecars were favored by the Army, so the sidecar production figures for 1917 and 1918 were 5,600 and 13,300 respectively (the 1919 sidecar total is unknown).

In contrast to Indian, Harley-Davidson didn't make such a large commitment to military production. Thus, they were able to farm the fertile fields of civilian riders and dealers who craved new motorcycles. The war, then, marked a turning point in the epic of Harley versus Indian.

The two companies had long differed in marketing strategies. Indian had been so successful so quickly that it practiced what economists call "pull demand," meaning that the superiority of the product would drive consumers into the dealerships. This worked well for Indian until 1915. But the Wigwam fell into the habit of treating its dealers like order takers who should be grateful to the all-knowing factory for the Indian franchise that guaranteed Mr. Dealer's success. In contrast, Harley-Davidson, in playing catch-up, practiced "push demand." This meant that Harley-Davidson had to deal with two sets of customers, dealers as well as riders. Dealers had to be convinced to handle Harleys. The ultimate arrogance for Indian was the abandonment of its dealers for the quick and sure profits of military business. Indian assumed its dealers would wait for the return of Indian to the civilian market. To a large extent, this didn't happen. Disgruntled dealers either quit the business for better opportunities, went broke while trying to hang on, or switched to other marques, especially Harley-Davidson.

The war also caused the total disruption of racing during 1917 and 1918. When racing resumed in 1919, Indian rider Gene Walker became practically unbeatable in the short races, where rider skill mattered more than long-haul reliability and team strategy.

1917
catalog cover. *"A new champion was born—a power plant that shattered the traditions of Herculean strength and enduring might come into being."*

Great Motorcycles, But More Bad Business

1920–1929

Nineteen twenty stands out as one of the brightest in the history of the Indian motorcycle. The new mid-sized V-twin Scout ushered in features that placed it well ahead of all rivals. So sound was this design and so strong was its acceptance, that the Scout became the basis of all subsequent V-twin Indian models right up until the very end. Although trouble lay ahead for Indian in the 1920s, these would be management and financial problems, not technical problems. The 600-cc Scout design and its legacies, the 1000-cc Chief, and 1200-cc Big Chief, gave the Indian company enough functional superiority to ride out the coming storm of mismanagement.

1920: The New Scout

The Indian lineup consisted of three basic models: the Powerplus single, the Powerplus twin, and the Scout. Variations in equipment such as lights versus no lights, resulted in additional model designations. For the

Circa 1926 ex-Curly Fredericks Powerplus racer. Somehow, Wigwam wizard Charles Franklin was able to extract more speed from Indian side-valve motors than Harley-Davidson could extract from eight-valve overheads. The board-track machines ran without a gearbox, so they had to be towed to a start. Racers began with a so-called flying start. A pace vehicle would flag the start once all contestants were evenly aligned. Owner: Peter Arundel.

1920 season, Charles Franklin made his greatest contribution to Indian engineering, the mid-sized, 37-ci (600-cc) V-twin Scout.

The side-valve Scout combined advanced engineering, surprising power, and unbeatable reliability, offering riders the best of both worlds—easy handling, plus enough power to ride as fast as permitted by most roads of 1920. As well as being a good seller, the new middleweight served as an entry-level model, which brought new riders into the game. Further, the Scout was the genesis for the larger Chief that followed it two years later and would carry on until the end of production in 1953. Franklin's side-valve twins were in production with major features intact for a period of 34 years, a remarkably long run. Surely, he was doing something right.

The Scout featured a semi-unit-construction powerplant with the transmission bolted to the back of the engine. An indestructible helical-gear primary drive, enclosed in a cast-aluminum housing and running in an oil bath, connected the engine and transmission. Prior to this time, most motorcycles around the world had used metal plates to connect engines and frames.

The Scout also differed by having a double-loop, rigid cradle frame, which provided a flat platform for mounting the engine/transmission powerplant package solidly. The motor was mounted from the left and right front, and the transmission from the middle rear. This three-point powerplant mounting avoided any twisting forces that might occur from mounting at four or more points.

Circa 1926 ex-Curly Fredericks Powerplus racer. The frame, but not the motor, of this machine is believed to be the one used by Curly Fredericks on August 21, 1926, at the Rockingham track near Salem, New Hampshire. There, on the 1-1/4-mile board track, Fredericks ran the all-time fastest motorcycle board track lap of 120.3 miles per hour. The Powerplus racers were close relatives of the standard road models, a good selling point for Indian dealers.

The Scout broke new ground with its valve gear as well. Instead of a single camshaft to operate all four valves, there were two camshafts, each operating both valves of its dedicated cylinder. Each camshaft had a single-lobe cam that operated both inlet and exhaust valves through pivoted cam followers or valve lifters.

The cylinders and cylinder heads were of the Powerplus style, cast in one piece and with a removable valve cap above each valve. Roller bearings were fitted to the connecting rod big end and to both the drive and pinion shafts. The flywheels were of one-piece, webbed construction, the outer rim of each flywheel encircling a beam that was drilled for crankshaft and main-shaft installation. The bore and stroke was 2-3/4x3-1/16 inches, yielding a displacement of 36.38 ci (596.16 cc); nominally the displacement was referred to as 37 ci or 600 cc.

The fully serviced Scout weighed 340 pounds. The maximum power output was only 11 horsepower, but the engine had a flat torque curve and was able to move the motorcycle up to about 55 miles per hour. A cruising

1924 Chief and sidecar. Following the success of the 1920 and 1921 Scouts, the Chief debuted as a bigger Scout in the 1922 lineup. The 1922 Chief was hailed as a trendsetter because of its 61-ci engine compared to rival 74-ci and larger models.

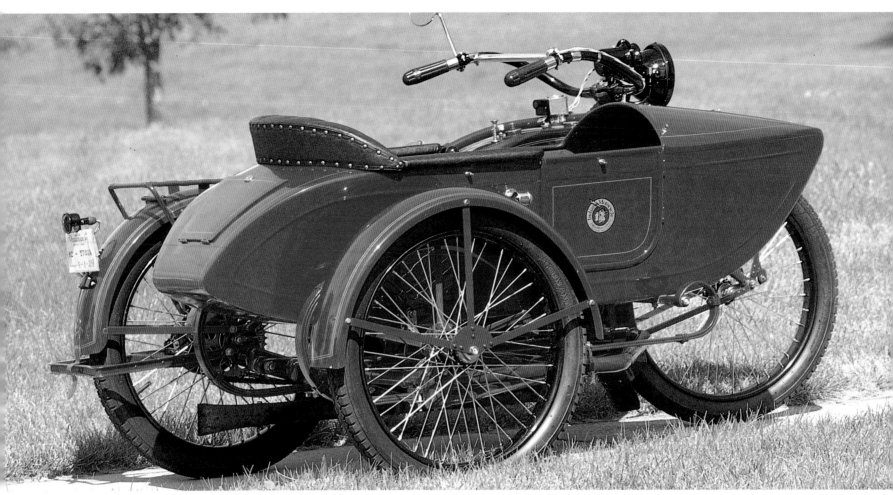

1924 Chief and sidecar. Indian pitched the 61-ci Chief and the 74-ci Big Chief as sidecar haulers, while touting the 37-ci Scout as the ideal solo, (i.e., single-track) motorcycle. In 1923, the 74-ci Big Chief appeared in the lineup and immediately became the company's biggest-selling model. The 61-ci Chief was offered through 1929 but the 74-ci Big Chief was always more popular. From 1930 on, only the 74-ci Chief was built. Restoration by owner Gene Harper.

speed of 45 miles per hour could be maintained, which in an era of mostly unpaved roads, was usually fast enough. A ride on a Scout left the impression of indestructibility. This proved true when the same clutch, gear-driven primary, and transmission were later used on the much more powerful 45-ci Scouts. In fact, in later years these components proved entirely adequate for strokers of up to 57 ci (934 cc).

So good was the brilliantly conceived Scout that many police departments were replacing their 1000-cc and 1200-cc bikes with the little 600-cc wonder.

The rest of the 1920 lineup consisted of the Powerplus single and the Powerplus twin. Variations in equipment such as lights versus no lights resulted in multiple model designations for the three machines.

Powerplus Changes

The Powerplus range was now a mature design that required only minor technical and styling improvements, these based on rider and dealer feedback. Indian management probably already had in mind a larger model based on the Scout layout, and if so, this strategy would have further reduced engineering effort on the Powerplus range. Most of the detail changes presented on the 1920 Powerplus models were also featured on the new Scout.

The front-fork bell cranks had new screw-down lubricators. The fork main frame and truss rods were new, as was the front fender and fender brace. The headlight was a new Solar model, and the headlight brackets were new. Nickel plating was applied to the handlebar, which had an integral fork bracket. The control wires were sheathed in leather. Tank filler openings were enlarged to 1-1/2 inches. A new exhaust-valve lifter was fitted, and both the gearshift and clutch levers had an integral metal knob.

A Splitdorf Aero magneto provided the sparks, and on the electric models a Splitdorf DU 1 generator provided system charging. Footbrake and clutch pedal pads were larger.

The muffler was different because it had to accommodate the new larger exhaust pipes. From the muffler extended twin tailpipes. Twin tailpipes were not shown in the early publicity photos or sales catalogs; however, twin tailpipes were mentioned in the initial press releases and are listed in parts books as 1920 items. On the 61-ci model, new cylinders had larger exhaust ports.

Competition

In April, Gene Walker set a series of world records at Daytona Beach. Walker's best one-way wind-assisted run was 114.17 miles per hour, and his two-way average of 103.56 miles per hour was a new world record. These marks, made on a 61-ci eight-valve, were the last officially sanctioned maximum-speed world records for an American-made motorcycle. Walker also set some American records on both eight-valve and Powerplus models.

Also in April, Albert "Shrimp" Burns became the first rider to win a national championship at a 100-plus–mile-per-hour pace on a "stock" machine, a Powerplus racer, at Beverly Hills, California (15-mile race).

In August, the Scout proved its surprising power by setting a 24-hour world's road record, covering 1,114 miles over a closed course in Australia. This was 250 miles more than the previous record set by Cannonball Baker on a 61-ci Indian Powerplus.

On September 19, 1920, near Cleveland, Ohio, "Shrimp" Burns again took to the saddle, this time establishing a new 10-mile dirt track record of 7 minutes, 53 seconds on one of Franklin's side-valve racers. While logging this 76-mile-per-hour average, Burns defeated Jim Davis on an eight-valve Harley-Davidson. How could a side-valve defeat an eight-valve, hemispherical, overhead-valve motor? One wonders even today at this turn of events, but it was to happen over and over under Franklin's genius.

In November, Herbert "Bert" LeVack set kilometer and mile records for England, at Brooklands, averaging 95.2 miles per hour. During the year Indian won 14 national championship races at distances of one through 50 miles, with total winning mileage of 200 miles. But Harley-Davidson won 511 miles of racing—though spread over only three races—all hotly contested and widely publicized national championships. So the 1920 racing season was a mixture of pride and disappointment for Indian.

1921: Harley-Davidson Racing Dominance

For the 1921 season the Powerplus single was dropped, reducing the Indian lineup from three basic models to two basic models, the Powerplus twin and the Scout. Optional electric lights and generator were new for 1921. No other significant external changes applied to the Powerplus series. The electrically equipped Scouts had a generator takeoff drive mounted above the clutch housing.

In 1921, Harley-Davidson won every national championship motorcycle race in the United States. Having proved its point—albeit at tremendous

1924 Chief and sidecar. New pull-action front forks had the axle and spring connections on opposite sides of the main fork structure so that upward wheel movement pulled the leaf springs downward.

1924 Chief and sidecar. *The emphasis on the Chief as a sidecar hauler is shown by the left side kickstarter. The kickstarter was mounted to the vertical frame tube behind the powerplant, so the kicker could be relocated to the right side. This helped in Britain where sidecars were on the left side of the motorcycle.*

1924 Chief and sidecar. *Typical Indian detailing of the era. Note the narrow pinstripes. These correct stripes are 3/64 inches wide, and are patterned after unrestored machines.*

expense—Harley-Davidson withdrew from factory-supported racing at the end of the season. Excelsior, the only serious racing rival to Indian and Harley, also deemphasized racing but for too few, not too many wins. Excelsior's "X" had a habit of bettering the previous years' winning speeds in race after race, but still found Indian and Harley faster.

Bert LeVack, riding a 61-ci Powerplus racer, won the longest race in England, a 500-miler at Brooklands. But the concrete oval didn't rival the Isle of Man TT in prestige. On the island, Indian won the team award for consistency, but here again this paled in comparison to winning outright. Neither outing had much impact on the isolated American motorcycling scene.

Prototype 1926 overhead-cam Prince. Engineer Charles Franklin was in tune with the transatlantic market, where lightweight models dominated sales. For the 1925 season, Franklin designed a 21-ci side-valve single-cylinder model dubbed the Prince. With the side-valve Prince launched, Franklin turned his attention to overhead-valve and overhead-cam versions. The overhead-valve Prince with pushrod valve actuation reached production, but the overhead-cam job didn't. Restoration by owner Woody Carson. David Jehu

1922: The Chief and Other News

Indian's big news for the 1922 season was the "big Scout," the 61-ci Chief. The Chief was regarded as a new genre proving that design sophistication was more important than cubic capacity. After all, Indian *already* had a 72-ci Powerplus (renamed the "Standard") and Harley-Davidson was in its second year of 74-ci (1200-cc) production.

In *Motorcycling and Bicycling* for September 7, 1921, the road tester put it this way: "Ever since Indian Scout rolled out along the highways and by-ways of the world, and won its place in the esteem of motorcyclists by its ability to deliver 100 percent satisfaction in every phase of motorcycling, be it utility, recreation, or competition, there has been an insistent question asked, 'Why not a big brother to this wonder model?'

"And now you may have it. Indian Chief, the last word in motorcycle construction and design—take it from me—is making its debut, to the vast throng who ride and who will ride motorcycles, as one of the 1922 models of the Hendee Mfg. Co.

"Indian Chief, Scout's big brother, is a wonderful motorcycle. Powered with a 61 inch engine, it is a marvel of power, speed, silence, and accessibility. All that a larger capacity motor will do, Indian Chief will do as well,

if not better. A reduction in the size of engines, a goal that has been ever in the minds of automobile engineers, and temporarily lost sight of by motorcycle engineers, with no reduction in power or speed, is a notable achievement in itself. A most promising sign that the motorcycle engine of the future must not necessarily be a hulking big twin . . ."

Beyond the Chief, changes to the rest of the Indian line for the 1922 season were minor. The Powerplus was renamed the "Standard" to keep buyers from believing these machines had more power than the newly launched 61 ci Chief models. The ever-popular Scout rounded out the 1922 lineup of three basic models.

The newly named Standard featured new front and rear fenders that were more deeply valanced. Both fenders were supported by new flat-strip braces instead of the earlier rod style braces. The rear fender was hinged to ease tire removal. The rear frame section featured a wider "horseshoe" to accommodate the wider rear fender. The taillight cable was routed outside the rear fender. In response to dealer demands for faster machines, aluminum pistons were offered on both the 61- and 72-ci versions.

Among the changes to the 1922 Scout was the labeling of the primary drive cover with "Hendee Manufacturing Co. Springfield Mass. U.S.A." Earlier covers had no writing, and of course the new Chief also had the label. On the Scout timing case cover, there was a new, removable oil pump, another upgrade courtesy of the Chief. Earlier Scout oil pumps had been cast integral with the cover.

The Scout frame was given a vertical seat post in order to work with the new sprung-seat-post arrangement. The seat post springing was a copy of a long-running Harley-Davidson feature.

Some 1920 and 1921 Scouts had experienced broken transmission cases in the area where the kickstarter mounted to the aluminum case. Since the Scout motor and transmission were bolted together as a single powerplant package, and the powerplant package had a fixed mounting in the

1926 Prince. Indian seemed to never tire of seeking a large market for low-cost, utilitarian motorcycles. The bicycle-like "motocycles" of Oscar Hedstrom were successful motorcycles for the masses, but Indian never again found the combination. This Prince represents Indian's fifth generation, aimed at the utility market and, to a lesser extent, the market for boys and women. Other low-buck efforts were the 1914 Little Twin, the 1916 Featherweight two-stroke, the 1917–1919 Light Twin, and the Powerplus singles of the late 1910s and early 1920s. Restoration by Bollenbach Engineering.

frame, the kickstarter could be mounted to the frame. So Indian solved the broken transmission case problem by mounting the Scout kickstarter to the seat mast.

Competition

With Harley-Davidson and Excelsior out of the game, Indian's national championships didn't carry much weight. One achievement was notable, more so in retrospect than at the time. On April 14, at the Beverly Hills 1-1/4-mile board track, Jim Davis rode an Indian to the fastest one mile ever recorded on the boards, 110.67 miles per hour.

1923: The Big Chief and Other Changes

Apparently, most Americans didn't agree with the earlier mentioned road tester who had envisioned the 1922 Chief as forerunner of future smaller but more efficient motorcycles. Answering the public's incessant cry for more power, Indian brought out the 74-ci (1200-cc) Big Chief for 1923. The Big Chief immediately took over the role of sales leader. Indian now had four basic models, the Standard, the Scout, the Chief, and the Big Chief.

Never stagnant, Indian made the following changes to the Scout and Chief. Tanks were changed to accommodate a side-mounted compression release rod. Luggage racks became optional equipment on the Scout and Chief. On the Scout, a cost-cutting measure saw the replacement of the aluminum switch box and built-in ammeter with a simple ammeter and separate switch. The Scout toolbox was moved from the luggage rack to the lower left side and was connected to the battery box with a special bracket.

One of the last changes in 1923 occurred in November: The company announced the change of its name from The Hendee Manufacturing Company to The Indian Motocycle Company (there was that word "motocycle" again!). The company took great pains to instruct its dealers how to use this mysterious "r-less" term. It was appropriate to use the term "motorcycle" when the term was isolated from the word "Indian," but when the two words were used together the "r" was to be omitted. Thus, the correct forms were: "Indian motocycle" and "the Indian is a good motorcycle . . ."

Paul Remaly

Paul Remaley and record-setting Scout.

The Motorcycle and Allied Trades Association stopped sanctioning long-distance road records in 1919 because they felt speed-limit violations were bad publicity. But of the American factories, only Harley-Davidson stayed out of the game.

In 1923, advertisements proclaimed any long-distance record worth having was held by the Henderson Four. Imagine the embarrassment of Henderson devotees when in May 1923 Paul Remaley rode a 600-cc Indian Scout from Tijuana, Mexico, to Blaine, British Columbia, in 46 hours and 58 minutes, breaking a Three-Flag record held by Wells Bennett on a 1300-cc Henderson Four. In June, Bennett lowered the Three Flag mark to 46 hours and 9 minutes. In July, Remaley added insult to injury with a Scout Three-Flag run of 43 hours and 21 minutes.

By August, Remaley had grown tired of the Three-Flag game and took aim at the transcontinental record of 6 days, 16 hours, and 13 minutes, another Henderson achievement. Remaley and the little Scout amazed motorcyclists by crossing the continent in 5 days, 17 hours, and 10 minutes, beating the Henderson time by over 22 hours. Shortly afterwards, Indian announced that it would no longer support record runs over public roads, due to its position as a major supplier to police departments.

1924: Changes and Competition

Changes to the 1924 Indian lineup were minimal. Again, the Indian showrooms fielded four basic models: the Standard, the Scout, the Chief, and the Big Chief. On the Scout, a running change was the single-line pin striping, which replaced the earlier double-line striping. A notable change to the Scout, Chief, and Big Chief occurred in mid-season when the front fork was changed from a push-action to a pull-action. A new front fender was installed on the late-season Scout, Chief, and Big Chief to accommodate the new fork.

On the racing scene, the move to smaller motors continued in 1924 with the aim of making racing safer. Gone were the famous 61-ci (1000-cc) eight-valve and F-Head Harleys and side-valve Indians. All national championships were limited to 30.5-ci (500-cc) machines. Of the six national

1926 Prince. The long rod by the side of the tank is the compression release, but there wasn't a lot of compression to relieve with an estimated 5.5:1 compression ratio. Snaking along from the tank to the right side of the engine are two oil-supply lines. Notice that there's no oil-return line. As in other motors of the era, the oil didn't circulate. Oil metering was just sufficient to replenish the oil consumed by the motor.

titles, Indian won two to Harley's four. Two popular racers, Indian's Gene Walker and Harley's Ray Weishaar (pronounced "Wisher") died in racing accidents.

1925: Standard Dropped, Prince Added

Missing from the 1925 lineup was the Standard, which despite its rear suspension had continuously declined in popularity. Working against the Standard was its ancient appearance and high saddle position. Harley

1926 Prince. Rider's-eye view shows the unlighted 80-mile-per-hour speedometer. Speedometers were the most popular accessory fitted to all Indian models. On the right side, from front to back, are the oil cap, oil hand pump, and gas cap. The oil hand pump was for rougher than average riding, like fast running, riding up long grades, or riding in long stretches of sand. If a rider was unsure about lubrication, he shut the throttle and glanced back. A puff of blue smoke meant everything was okay. If there was no answering puff, the rider pulled up the hand pump knob half a stroke and then pushed it slowly and firmly to the bottom. Such Indian "total-loss" oiling meant there was never more than half a cup of oil in the bottom end, even in the mighty big twins.

1926 Prince. The 21-ci side-valve motor put out about six horsepower, good enough for nearly 60 miles per hour and with a miserly fuel consumption rate of 55 miles per gallon. The oil hand pump line to the left crankcase is shown, the generator near the top of the engine, and the magneto near the bottom of the engine.

dealers had also made some mileage by claiming the Indian spring frame caused chains to be thrown.

The Scout got a new saddle suspension, which was changed from seat-post springing to conventional coil saddle springs. The Scout was also fitted with new removable cylinder heads (previously the heads and cylinders were one-piece castings), and the pattern of the Scout's cooling fins was changed from radial to fore-and-aft.

Aluminum "B" motors for Scouts and Chiefs were introduced in August 1925. These motors offered higher performance and greater resistance to overheating and were listed by Indian until 1935 when they were replaced by "Y" motors. Among the principle differences between standard and "B" motors were aluminum pistons and looser clearances throughout. This latter improvement reduced friction and minimized the potential for

motor seizure at sustained high speeds.

The stalwarts of Indian's line, the Scout, Chief, and Big Chief, received only a few detail changes, the most obvious being optional, larger cross-section "balloon" tires and a new clutch housing label that read "Indian Motocycle Company." This change also may have applied to late-season 1924 models.

Nineteen twenty-five also saw the introduction of the new 21.35-ci (350-cc), side-valve, single-cylinder Prince. Records don't exist concerning Indian's engineering deliberations during this era, but Harley-Davidson records shed some light on Indian's decision to produce a 350-cc single. Following a tour of Europe and Australia in 1924, Harley-Davidson's three Davidson brothers and Bill Harley decided the export market was ripe for a Harley-Davidson 350-cc side-valve single. Either Indian did a separate market study that led to the same conclusion, or Indian got wind of Harley's plans and decided to join the battle. If nothing else, Indian likely reasoned, its entry into the lightweight battle might keep Harley-Davidson from gaining an important commercial advantage.

Indian announced its new 350-cc side-valve single, the Prince, shortly after Harley debuted its own. Both companies followed up a few months later with overhead-valve versions. Judging from the surviving examples from each company, Harley-Davidson must have been more successful than Indian. Exports for both companies suffered a catastrophic drop-off after the British raised motorcycle tariffs to Empire nations. Harley-Davidson records indicate that Milwaukee lost all of its substantial export business—about 40 percent of Harley-Davidson sales—almost immedi-

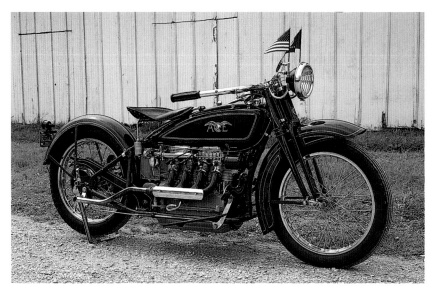

1927 Ace. In February 1927, Indian purchased the floundering Ace motorcycle company. During the spring, Indian began to manufacture the Ace, with Indian Red the standard color but with Ace Blue still available by request. This Ace has the typical wheels and tires the Ace company used. Very soon after Indian took over Ace production, the fours were fitted with smaller diameter wheels and larger cross section "balloon" tires. The single front down tube and lower front horizontal tubing of the Ace were retained as the four-cylinder model evolved from the 1927 "Ace" to the 1928 "Indian Ace" to the early-1929 "Indian Four."

Motorcyclists (F.I.C.M.) due to alleged timing-equipment irregularities.

Higher Indian speeds were aided by the development work of Charles Franklin. In 1925, he was busy pursuing racing development along two lines. The recent introduction of tetra-ethyl lead as a gasoline additive permitted higher compression ratios, which in turn was supposed to spell the end of competitive side-valve racers—a prediction which, over the long haul, would prove true. Following British and European trends, Franklin began experimenting with a new series of 45-ci four-valve (two valves per cylinder) overhead-valve twins to replace the old 61-ci eight-valve twins (four valves per cylinder).

Concurrent with this new line of development, Franklin sur-

ately. Undoubtedly, Indian also suffered a great loss from the trade war between the United States and the British Empire. Sales of the Prince single were disappointing, perhaps because there just wasn't a big enough market for both Indian and Harley-Davidson. Responding to the loss of all foreign business, Indian closed the London Branch it had operated for almost 20 years. Indian achieved further cost cutting by selling off the East Springfield equipment and machinery. Hard times had arrived for the American motorcycle industry fully five years before the great depression.

Competition and Racing Developments

The Motorcycle and Allied Trades Association (M & ATA) was the governing body for motorcycle racing in the United States. The organization's indecision about big racing motorcycles was evidenced in 1925 when the 61-ci class was reinstated to national championship status. Harley-Davidson won all eight big-motor titles, while Indian captured five of the six championships for 30.50-ci machines.

In October, Paul Anderson rode a 45-ci Indian featuring a new overhead-valve design to establish a French record of 135.71 miles per hour, with a fastest one-way run of 159.08 miles per hour, at Arpajon Speedway. The record wasn't recognized by the Federation Internationale des Clubs

prised himself with the power he was able to extract from the 61-ci side-valve design that supposedly was now unsuitable for racing. These Franklin side-valve racers became the front-line troops in the racing war with Harley-Davidson's eight-valve overheads, and continued success in this match-up was especially rewarding in light of the fact that the racing Indians were of the same general layout as the road models.

One of these racing side-valve Indian big twins was timed at 117 miles per hour on Australia's Sellick Beach in 1925. This was less than 2 miles per hour slower than the official world's record established by a 61-ci overhead-valve Brough-Superior.

1926

Following recent custom, changes to the 1926 road models were minor. A notable change occurring in the middle of the 1926 production run was the option of unpainted crankcases, primary drive housings, and transmissions. Previously, these assemblies had been painted in the dominant motorcycle color, typically Indian Red. A stop light was available for the first time, but only as an accessory.

On the Scout, the switchbox with built-in ammeter returned, having previously been used only on the 1922 model. Scout cylinder cooling fins

Long Board-Track Action

The short board tracks called motordromes fell from favor between 1912 and 1915 because of accidents and the public's dwindling curiosity about motorcycles. Among the early board tracks was a design exception, the mile-long Playa Del Rey track in the coastal town of the same name just west of Los Angeles. This was the only one of the early board tracks designed primarily for car racing.

Promoter and track builder Jack Prince, who had designed and built Playa Del Rey and all the motordrome motorcycle tracks around the country, escaped the motordrome backlash by building his second long track with car racing in mind. This was the 2-mile-long Speedway Park at Chicago, which opened in 1915 before 85,000 spectators who turned out to watch a 500-mile car race. The Chicago speedway was a roaring success. Other long board tracks opened soon at Tacoma, Washington; Omaha, Nebraska; Des Moines, Iowa; Sheepshead Bay (Brooklyn), New York; Cincinnati, Ohio; Beverly Hills, Fresno, Cotati, and San Francisco, California; and Kansas City, Kansas. These tracks ranged from 1-1/4 to 2 miles. The Tacoma Speedway lasted from 1915 through 1922, but most of the rest failed commercially within a couple of years.

The next long board tracks were more successful. The 1-1/4–mile Altoona, Pennsylvania, track opened in 1923 and ran races until 1931, making it the longevity champion of the boards. The Laurel, Maryland, track ran only a year, but the Rockingham Speedway track at Salem, New Hampshire, ran from 1925 through 1928.

Although the long board tracks were designed for car racing, many important motorcycle events were staged on them. These included the first sanctioned 100-mile-per-hour speed record at Playa Del Rey in 1912 (Excelsior, Lee Humiston), the 1915 300-Mile National Championship at Chicago, the 1919 100-Mile

This is a scene from a circa 1915 Chicago speedway race, but it typifies the long board-track action that was more prominent in the 1920s. *Geoff Hockley.*

National Championship at Sheepshead Bay, the first motorcycle race won at a 100-plus–mile-per-hour average at Fresno in 1921 (Harley-Davidson, Otto Walker), the 1923 100-Mile National Championship at Kansas City, and the 1925 100-Mile National Championship at Altoona. This is only a partial listing.

Of all the original board-track sites, only Rockingham still operates, now as the famous dirt horse track. Today, apartment dwellers in Playa Del Rey doubtless wonder why one of the short streets is called Speedway Avenue.

were deeper and wrapped around the exhaust ports. Cone-type exhaust pipes were slipped over the exhaust nipples, so there were no large exhaust union nuts. On the Prince, the unpopular wedge-shaped tank was replaced by a new tank bearing the same shape as the Scout's, and the upper frame tube was accordingly reshaped from a straight section to a curved section.

Competition

In January 1926, Johnny Seymoure set American 30.50-ci and 61-ci records at Daytona Beach, Florida, of 112.63 miles per hour and 132 miles per hour respectively. These records weren't recognized internationally because Indian was no longer a political force in the international sanctioning body. With the collapse of overseas markets, the lack of international sanctions meant little, if anything at all, to commercial success. By comparison, the official international record in the 1000-cc class was way down,

119 miles per hour by Bert LeVack on a JAP-powered (J. A. Prestwich) Brough-Superior. In fairness, it should be noted that Seymoure ran in one direction only, as permitted under American rules, so he was afforded the opportunity for wind assistance.

Later that year, on August 21, 1926, Curly Fredericks set a record destined never to be broken. On the mile-long Rockingham board track at Salem, New Hampshire, Fredericks turned the all-time fastest board track lap at 120.3 miles per hour. His mount was a 61-ci, side-valve, Altoona twin with dual Zenith carburetors.

Indian had the best racing season of the big three brands, winning eight of the 12 solo national championships in 1926. The national championships that year were run in three classes, 30.50 ci, 45 ci, and 61 ci. In all cases these were maximum-displacement classes, hence a 30.50-ci bike could compete in the 45-ci class. The 45-ci class was instigated at the

request of Excelsior, which alone among the big three made a standard road bike of that displacement, the Super-X. Ironically, the first 45-ci national title went to Jim Davis on a 30.50-ci Indian.

In 1926, according to one story, Indian built a batch of 26 Franklin-designed 45-ci overhead-valve motors for competition. Another story has it that Indian built 20 of these motors between 1925 and 1930. Take your pick. In any case, these 45-ci overheads were different from the Paul Anderson machine run in France in 1925. Most of these new 45s were fitted to hillclimbing frames—a very popular sport at the time that enjoyed considerable support from the big three. Two of the 1926 45-ci overheads were mounted in track machines and at least one was outfitted for road racing or "miniature TT" racing. (This latter form of sport was named after the Isle of Man TT races. American TT rac-

1927 30.50-ci racer. The taped hook behind the engine was a brace for the rider's right leg while broadsliding in left turns. One shudders to think what kind of injuries this might cause in a spill. Power output was 25–30 horsepower, and the top speed on a mile track was about 90 miles per hour. Although this particular machine has an iron cylinder head, an aluminum head was available. These Class A racers had compression ratios of 12:1 to 14:1 and used special fuel. Owner: R. L. Jones. Mark Mitchell; assistance by *Indian Motorcycle Illustrated*

ing was a precursor to the scrambles racing of the 1960s, which in turn gave way to motocross. All TT courses had to have at least one right turn and one left turn, and at least one jump. These TT 45-ci overheads burned alcohol and sported a compression ratio of 15:1!)

1927:
Indian's Best Motor and the Origin of the Indian Four

Probably the best engine Indian ever built was the 45-ci V-twin introduced during the 1927 season. This was, of course, an enlarged version of the earlier 37-ci Scout motor. Introduced originally as the Police Special on

1927 30.50-ci racer. From 1924 through 1938 the American factories provided single-cylinder overhead-valve racers. In 1924, only the 30.50-ci size was built, but in later years 21.35-ci singles were also raced. This example is believed to be one of four such racers Indian built in 1927. All American flat-track racing was done without brakes until 1969. Owner: R. L. Jones. Mark Mitchell; assistance by Indian Motorcycle Illustrated

the standard Scout wheelbase, the "45" motor served out its life as the muscle of the longer-wheelbase versions and the famous Series 101 Scout. The new 45 was a happy combination of bore, stroke, and other factors, and the motor seemed to work better than it should have. The "Police Special" designation was important not only for marketing to police departments but also because cop bikes in those days had a speed image. Motor assembly instructions for both Indians and Harleys specified larger clearances throughout on police models, as in racers.

Indian's other new engine was its four-cylinder, which originated when the company bought out the Ace motorcycle company in 1927. The Ace had existed as an independent manufacturer from late 1919, and was designed by William Henderson. Bill Henderson had made the Henderson marque famous and then sold out to Ignaz Schwinn, builder of the Excelsior line.

Some of the Ace's major design aspects were retained throughout the production of the Indian Ace and the Indian Four from 1928 through 1942. The bore and stroke remained constant at 2-3/4x3-1/4 inches for a displacement of 77.21 ci (1265 cc). The Ace layout used from 1927 through 1935 produced an estimated 30 horsepower, sufficient for about a 75-miles-per-hour top speed. Except for the 1936 and 1937 models, all four-cylinder heads contained overhead inlet valves and cylinders contained side-mounted (and inverted) exhaust valves. For 1936 and 1937, this arrangement was reversed. Fours from 1927 through 1929 had three main bearings, and from 1930 through 1942 had five main bearings. But all Indian four-cylinder models had the same crankshaft oil passages, with oil pumped to the connecting rods from the front, center, and rear main crankshaft bearings only. All Indian four-cylinder models used essentially the same transmission. There were only two significant gearbox changes through the lifespan of the four-cylinder models: a higher (numerical) gear ratio for second-gear introduced in 1927, and a higher (numerical) overall gear ratio in 1933, which continued through 1942. It was necessary to spin the later Fours faster because of their increasing weight.

Two new engines in one year allowed Indian to launch a double-pronged attack on the market. This gave Indian a "full line" of singles, twins, and a four, as Indian's magazine advertisements proudly proclaimed. All Ace tooling was moved during early 1927. Beginning in May 1927, blue (standard) or red (optional) machines carrying the traditional "Ace" tank emblem were built at the Wigwam.

Indian's full product line performed as well on the track as on the sales floor, as the company took five out of the nine national titles. The 30.50-ci class was replaced by the new 21.35-ci class which was dictated by the entry of Indian and Harley-Davidson into this market. Indian won two of the "21" class titles and Harley won the other three. The Wigwam copped both 61-ci class titles and split the two 45-ci national crowns with Super-X.

1928: No Annual Models

From 1928 through 1931, Indian had a policy of no annual models with the stated intention of bringing out all improvements as soon as possible rather than waiting for a formal launch date. Strictly speaking, there were no 1928, 1929, 1930, and 1931 models. Despite this policy, improvements still seemed to be made annually and collectors still refer to the different configurations by model-year.

At the top of the line, the "1928-model" red "Indian Ace" replaced the 1927-model Indian-built Ace and was the first Indian-built four to be featured in sales literature. At the other end of the line, the Prince single was given a shapely 101-style tank. Other changes were minor until mid-season, when all models received a front brake.

Another mid-season announcement proclaimed the new Series 101 Scout, which was achieved by lengthening the wheelbase about three inches and lowering the saddle almost two inches. A new more graceful tank was also fitted. Now, the happy combination of factors that had made the 45-ci

1928 Series 101 Scout. The Series 101 Scout was about three inches longer than the original Scout series, and the saddle was about two inches lower. The result: an incredible combination of stability and agility. These bikes are still used for stunt riding. This Scout has optional low "Sport" handlebars. Restoration by owner Roger Long.

motor just right, was joined by the new 101 frame that, too, was just right. The 101 frame and fork geometry combined stability and agility in a way that no design before or since has equalled. Even into the 1990s, a few Indian 101 Scouts soldier on as stunt-riding mounts in locations around the world.

On all models, front brakes were provided for the first time as a running change. The earliest 1928-model publicity photos appeared in the August magazines, and these photos showed all models without front brakes. Early sales catalogs also showed this configuration, but later 1928 catalogs showed all models with front brakes.

Despite building good motorcycles, Indian stayed mired in financial trouble. The reason was its constant meddling in areas outside its motorcycle expertise. Non-motorcycle production items included automobile shock absorbers and outboard motors, both of which proved unprofitable. Central to these excursions was the makeup of Indian's controlling management group whose members were neither motorcycle enthusiasts nor professional manufacturing managers. They were instead financiers whose view of the Wigwam was that it was a production facility, and whose view of the Indian company was that anything that was built there could be sold. They didn't understand that among Indian's most valuable assets were its marketing know-how and its person-to-person contacts in the highly specialized motorcycle field. To worsen matters, a few genuine crooks took over the management in the late 1920s and milked the company's treasury. By the end of the roaring twenties, Indian was perilously close to shutting down.

Competition

During this era Harley-Davidson lost interest in racing partly because it had established its image as the fastest brand on the highways by consistently beating Indian and Excelsior on the racetrack. From 1922 through 1925 and again in 1928 Harley-Davidson did not field factory-supported teams. Consequently, Indian won all the national championship races in 1928. The standout day of the 1928 racing season was August 4. On the

Rockingham (Salem), New Hampshire, mile board track, Bill Minnick, Jim Davis, and Curly Fredericks won several races with 45-ci overhead twins, including national championships in both the 45-ci and 61-ci classes. The Franklin-designed 45 overheads thus displaced the Wigwam's historic eight-valve overhead twins and side-valve twins as the fastest mounts in the Indian stable.

1929: Good Decisions, Bad Decisions

At a time when Indian should have been overtaking Harley-Davidson, Indian was taken over. Persons untroubled by ethical considerations were in charge of Indian's present and future. One of the new management group's more ambitious plans was to use excess Wigwam capacity to build outboard motors. Apparently, they reasoned that the Indian name would help sell outboards, or perhaps they reasoned that selling was a small job compared to manufacturing. There also may have been personal reasons having nothing to do with the prospects for Indian success, as will be related later. At any rate, Indian purchased the Hartford Outboard Motor Company in 1929, and set itself up in the outboard motor business.

The outboard motor project was just one of several non-motorcycle efforts that were financial flops. From a 1941 report presented to then-President E. Paul du Pont: "During 1928 and 1929 the company engaged itself in the manufacture and distribution of lines not directly related to its principal products. These so-called unrelated lines included outboard motors, shock-absorbers, electric refrigerators, ventilators, and automobiles, and the engaging in the manufacture and sale of these lines resulted in a decrease in the working capital position of the company of approximately $1,250,000 . . ."

On the motorcycle side of the ledger, things were considerably more cheery. The Prince single, a poor seller from the outset, was dropped from the range. Among motorcycle changes the most obvious were those introduced on the Four. This machine was now the "Indian Four" instead of the "Indian Ace," and accordingly, the traditional Indian leaf-spring front fork displaced the Ace parallelogram or "springer" fork similar to the Harley-Davidson fork. Although the Ace-style single front down tube was maintained, and with it the Ace front portion of the lower frame tubes, the rest of the frame was shaped like that of the Series 101 Scout. These hybrid part-Indian, part-Ace frames were used in the early-1929 series. Also part of the early-1929 series makeover was the between-the-rails Series 101 Scout tank, minus the unneeded oil compartment and associated hardware.

During the 1929-model production run, Indian switched over to a completely Indian-style frame for the Four, effective with motor number EA-101. Despite oft-repeated Indian folklore, the 1929 through 1931 Indian Fours did not use the Series 101 Scout frame. No single part of the Four frames of this era will interchange with the equivalent Series 101 Scout frame part. All frame tubing on the 1929–1931 Fours is larger in diameter than the corresponding tubing on the Series 101 Scout. Analogous forgings are therefore not the same in the Four as in the Series 101 Scout. Granted, the frames of the two models look almost identical, even to the point that both models have the same wheelbase. But the look-alike aspect was a styling decision by Indian. Given that the Ace preceded the Series 101 Scout, and that the rear portion of the "Indian Four" frame was so similar to that of the "Indian Ace," the Series 101 Scout frame would seem to have been copied from the four-cylinder model rather than the Four frame being copied from the Series 101.

Changes to all models included drop-center rims (replaced clinchers), newly shaped tapered-roller-bearing wheel hubs, and from June 1929 carburetor bodies that were die stamped instead of cast.

As in 1928, Indian won all national championship races. These were the only two consecutive years that a single brand won all national titles. But it was really no contest because the Harley-Davidson factory wasn't playing the racing game.

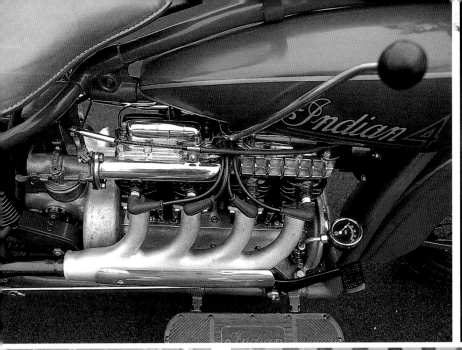

The Dark Ages

1930–1933

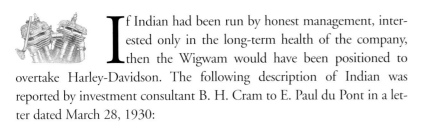

If Indian had been run by honest management, interested only in the long-term health of the company, then the Wigwam would have been positioned to overtake Harley-Davidson. The following description of Indian was reported by investment consultant B. H. Cram to E. Paul du Pont in a letter dated March 28, 1930:

MANUFACTURING: . . . very definite savings are being effected throughout the plant, while at the same time efficiency and morale are both markedly improved.
SALES: Dealers of inferior quality have been replaced with more active and better financed representatives and many additions to both the domestic and foreign dealer body have been made . . . The step-up in sales to municipalities for police work is particularly gratifying. Sales . . . for the period January 1, 1930, to March 26, 1930, were three times the amount of sales for the similar period of 1929. . .

1929 Four. From mid-1929, the Four was built with a twin-front-down-tube frame that strongly resembles the Model 101 Scout frame (the Four frame had larger tubing and forgings throughout). From a 1929 Indian Four catalog: "The utmost in motorcycle performance, beauty, and comfort . . . Smooth flowing power that speaks in a whisper compared to other motorcycles. Remember—four cylinders! The Indian Four needs no salesman." Owner/restorer Paul Pearce.

ADVERTISING AND PUBLICITY: An advertising campaign of national scope was inaugurated with the full-page *Saturday Evening Post* advertisement of March 15. The full campaign will include advertising in 15 magazines . . . . These magazines have a combined circulation of 6,716,600 copies . . . .

Top Left
1929 Four. Improvements for 1930 included new, high-turbulence cylinder heads, new pistons, new second-gear ratio for improved pickup, and new clutch plates. There are two housings for the inlet valves, and each housing has a long spring-loaded "tobacco can" door, which is lifted to squirt oil over the rocker-arm pivot points. The owner of this Four has opted for black-painted cylinders, a practical move because the factory practice of nickel plating leads to rapid rusting. The oil gauge was near the brake pedal, which meant many riders didn't pay enough attention to oil pressure. The gauge should read about 50 pounds per square inch when starting up from cold and when running at any speed above idle. Oil pressure can drop to 10 or 15 pounds per square inch when idling on a hot day.

Top Right
1929 Four. This typical Corbin-manufactured Indian accessory speedometer of the 1930s lacks internal illumination. Riders wanting a lighted speedometer bought an accessory light that bolted to the top frame tube near the speedometer clamp. Internally illuminated speedometers became available in 1932. The red hand is the maximum speed hand, which returns to zero when the rider pushes the reset button on the speedometer's left side. Speedometers became standard equipment on all Indians in 1938, except for on the low-cost Junior Scout.

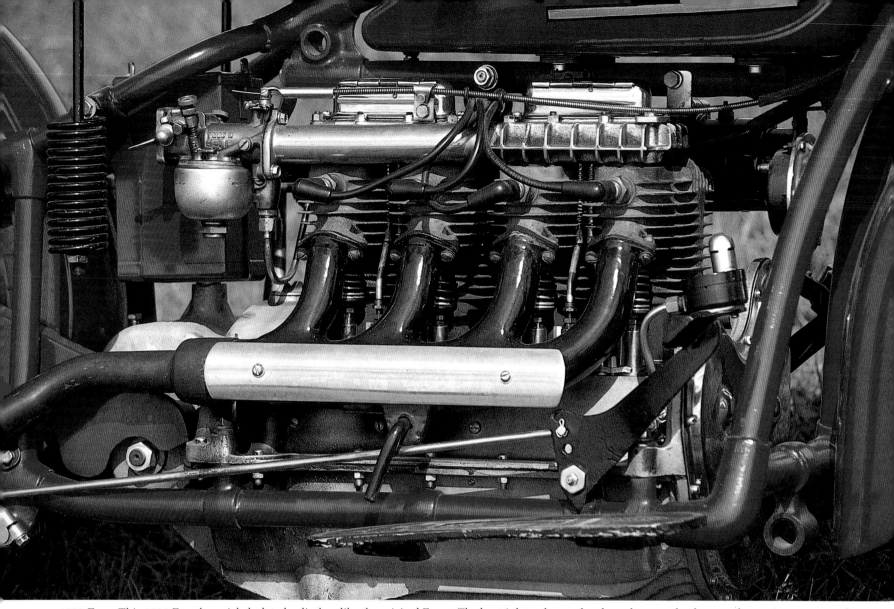

1930 Four. *This 1930 Four has nickel-plated cylinders like the original Fours. The bent inlet-valve pushrods and exposed exhaust-valve springs are great fun to watch at idle, or for a friend to watch while riding alongside. The valve mechanism tended to let oil out and dirt in. The Schebler carburetor is typical of those used on Indians from 1916 through 1940. In 1941, the Schebler name changed to Linkert. Scheblers and Linkerts are essentially identical. Restoration by owner Woody Carson.*

NEW MODELS: Improvements in design and equipment have taken place in all models. While this has had its inevitable effect on production (as to delays) it has enhanced the salability of the product considerably...

PRODUCTION: When the new executives assumed control of Indian, a house cleaning resulted as outlined in our former report. In order to visualize some of the progress made in actual production, the following figures representing monthly motorcycle output since November 1929 will be of value: November 1929—285, December 1929—287, January 1930—666, February 1930—934, March 1930 (to March 26)—1,451.

FINANCES: All bank loans and trade acceptances have been liquidated, placing the company in excellent condition to receive the advantage of purchase of material on the soundest of credit terms.

EARNINGS: . . . the prospects are even more clearly indicated for improvement, since, in addition to expanding motorcycle production, the outboard motor manufacture will soon contribute its share to Indian's earnings.

ADMINISTRATION: Present executives are energetically pursuing all sound methods of strengthening Indian's industrial and financial position through up-to-date engineering design, careful manufacturing, and pro-per ex-ploitation of products. . .

NEW DEVELOPMENTS: An event of extreme importance in our opinion, embracing exceptional potential possibilities, occurred when on March 14, 1930, Louis H. Coatalen, designer of international repute, became a director and consulting engineer of the Indian Motocycle Company . . . Mr. Coatalen, it might be mentioned, is best known in connection with the design of Sunbeam motor cars, marine engines, motorcycles, aircraft engines, the R-34 (British dirigible), and the Sunbeam Silver Bullet, special racing car driven at Daytona Beach by Kaye Don. . .

1930 Four. *The rather ambitious title of "instrument panel" was used for the ammeter and switch combination. High and low headlight beams were selected with the switch.*

permitted to keep the balance of any shares left over after negotiating the sale of the Coatelen rights. Obviously, this maneuver could lead to internal money laundering, a covert "share the wealth" plan among various members of the board. The excess money was "free," so to speak and could be pocketed without further accountability. E. Paul du Pont pressed his attack strongly and was able to force out the previous management team, who feared legal prosecution if du Pont didn't get his way.

E. Paul du Pont was an engineer by education and experience, and fully capable of running Indian efficiently. But he had too many irons in the financial fires to become consumed in the details of Indian's everyday management. For that task he brought in Loren F. "Joe" Hosley, former production manager at DuPont Motors, builders of the DuPont automobile. Hosley changed production methods to reduce the dependence on a large materials inventory. He also substantially reduced overhead and operating expenses. After only one month of management by the E. Paul du Pont and Loren "Joe" Hosley team, the outboard motor business was recognized as a flop and attempts to sell it were begun.

GENERAL: The uniqueness of the motorcycle industry is again given emphasis in that unlike passenger car manufacture, there is virtually no used vehicle problem, and little competition, and dealers almost universally operate at a profit with consequently much less dealer mortality than is the case with motor car dealers, a condition which automatically insures splendid dealer morale. In our opinion, Indian has, in a very short time, made most remarkable strides forward in its march to reinstate itself in its proper industrial niche.

Based on the Cram report, E. Paul du Pont sold the controlling interest in the DuPont automobile company to Indian. He and his brother Francis also bought large blocks of Indian stock, with Francis investing more than E. Paul. Indian looked like a good speculative stock.

The old Indian board overlooked one danger to their little club: E. Paul du Pont was no fool.

On April 23, E. Paul visited the Wigwam and concluded that the company suffered from lack of proper management due to President Bolles spending most of his time in New York without sufficient delegated authority in Springfield. E. Paul also observed that Indian was way behind in its accounts payable, with the result that some suppliers would only deal with Indian on a cash basis. Stock records indicated that a block of stock valued at $106,000 had been issued for cash, but the money couldn't be found. The purchase of Coatelen patent rights was arranged by a member of the Indian Board of Directors, who went bargaining with 50,000 shares of Indian stock and was

1930: Problems with the Chief

Design and quality-control problems plagued the Chief during this era. E. Paul du Pont compared his personal Chief to a Harley-Davidson 74 and found the Harley to be smoother running. In a July 17, 1930, letter to Hosley, du Pont wrote: ". . . to convince yourself of this, put the two machines side by side on a stand and start the motors. As they speed up, the Indian will be observed to vibrate so badly that it slides backwards on the floor, and any attempt to hold it is painful to the hand; whereas the Harley stays more or less where it is placed at any engine speed."

There were also instances of bearings going to pieces and flywheels exploding. To overcome these problems, Indian installed new crankshafts, new flywheels, and used a different balancing factor.

In the rest of the line-up, changes in minor details were the rule for 1930. An exception was the Four, which was given the important functional *continued on page 60*

E. Paul du Pont

E. Paul du Pont took an active interest in Indian engineering problems. He kept a stable of Indian models at his estate and provided written reports on deficiencies. E. Paul even studied engineering drawings and made suggestions. Here are his comments in a September 27, 1930, letter sent to engineer Charles Franklin:

> I have carefully looked over the tracing for the automatic oil pump, and my comments will be as follows: I understand that the pressure of the oil from the tank will be against the bushing on the shaft which comes through from the gear case. Do you not think that there would be danger of oil leaking into the case when the machine is left standing for a long period? If the general space inside of the pump could be maintained full from the discharge instead of from the intake, this might be obviated.
>
> I also observe, if I interpret the drawing correctly, that the slanting plate which operates the oil pump plunger is pivoted on the edge as in the present design. This causes the spring of the plunger to press at all times against the operation of the piston, i.e., the regulating piston. I doubt if the apparatus can be made to work unless the design is changed in such a way that this pivot is in the center of the plate and not at the edge, so that the action of the two plunger springs will tend to neutralize one another instead of always pushing one way . . .
>
> Referring to the matter of the plunger springs, I do not believe it will be possible to get sufficient pressure of oil from the valves to oppose the action of these springs, and that the apparatus as now laid out would not operate. I will make further comments on this at a later date.

In an October 7, 1930, letter to plant manager Loren Hosley, E. Paul continued his evaluation of the proposed throttle-actuated oil pump.

> I wish to call attention to the oil pump. I believe no time whatever should be lost in getting the throttle-actuated oil pump. I looked over the job as laid out by Mr. Franklin, and observe that he has rather expensive construction. If you could drop up there and take a look at the Harley-Davidson device it might be possible to begin at this point to make something that is not so expensive to build that we lose profit on the motorcycle. When you see it, you will know what I mean.

Entering the Indian scene in 1930 was new president E. Paul du Pont. Mr. du Pont, on the left, shows *Motorcyclist* editor Chet Billings the motorcycle that du Pont built as a boy in 1903. *Motorcyclist.*

Did President du Pont really affect Indian design and engineering, or did the Indian staff just politely accept his counsel and then go their own way? The author believes E. Paul du Pont was a real influence. According to his son Stephen, E. Paul personally laid out many of the engineering drawings of the military Model 841 shaft-drive transverse V-twin. Additionally, Stephen said E. Paul "had to prop up" G. Briggs Weaver, Indian's titular engineering chief from the mid-1930s on.

Steve du Pont proved to be a chip off the old block when, as leader of the engineering department in the early 1940s, he was instrumental in the design of the big-base racing Scout.

Right
1930 ex-Tom Paradise factory hillclimber. *The Indian, Harley-Davidson, and Excelsior factories supported a circuit of national championship hillclimbers during the late 1920s and in 1930, Excelsior's last season. Special rigs like this one and the factory Harleys and Excelsiors ran in no-holds-barred Class A events featuring factory-salaried riders. Indian and Harley stayed in the game until WWII. Typical hills were sloped about 45 degrees and up to 300 feet long. Owner: R. L. Jones.* Mark Mitchell; assistance by *Indian Motorcycle Illustrated*

Charles B. Franklin

Irishman Charles B. Franklin was a well-respected racer from 1908 through 1914, during which period he competed in every Isle of Man TT road race. He was known for the careful preparation of his motorcycles, which never broke down. His best race was the 1911 Isle of Man TT, when as a member of the Indian team he finished second to teammate Oliver Godfrey. According to historian Peter Hartley, in his book *Bikes At Brooklands,* in August 1911 at the Brooklands concrete track in England, Franklin made an important discovery. After welding a lump of metal in the combustion chamber roof of his F-Head Indian, he accidentally fell upon the squish principle of combustion chamber turbulence.

Chief Engineer Charles B. Franklin left Indian in 1930. Franklin designed both the Scout and the Chief, the latter remaining in continuous production for 32 years, with the same basic engine design.

In 1915, Franklin became the manager of the Indian depot in Dublin. The following year, he moved to the United States and joined the Indian engineering department. By this time, Indian's original designer, Oscar Hedstrom, had left the company, and the Hedstrom-designed inlet-over-exhaust motors had been replaced by the new line of Powerplus side-valve motors.

Franklin quickly became the dominant force in the engineering department. His 1920 600-cc side-valve Scout was a breakaway concept conceived as an integrated design from hub to hub. The Scout paved the way for the 1922 1000-cc Chief and the 1923 1200-cc Big Chief, the latter surviving until the company's end in 1953. Franklin also was a major player in the racing game. His uncanny ability to extract power from side-valve engines produced the spectacle of Indian side-valve twins out-running Harley-Davidson eight-valve overheads! The Franklin-designed Scout and Chief were so successful that Harley-Davidson did the then unthinkable—they switched to the side-valve layout during 1929 and 1930.

Franklin left Indian in 1930 due to poor health, and died two years later at 46. In their day, the 1953 Chiefs, despite archaic technical specifications that were rooted in 1920, were surpassed only by BMW opposed twins for long-distance cruising. The beautiful last-of-the-line 1953 Chiefs thus served as a tribute to Charles Franklin's design talent.

continued from page 57

improvement of a five-main-bearing crankshaft. Previously, the Four crankshaft was supported by only three main bearings.

There were two running changes on late-1930 models. Chromium trim was introduced in accord with a worldwide trend, and a new headlight with a chromium-plated embossed rim was installed. Indian claimed a 300 percent improvement in lighting as a result of the headlight change. A flexible (helical wound) "armored" taillight cable was fitted. On November 25, the company announced that frame numbers had been initiated—earlier Indians had a motor number only.

On the Chief, cast-aluminum tanks were installed. On the Four, larger front wheel and sidecar wheel spokes were fitted.

1931

This was the end of the no-annual-models era, a marketing experiment that didn't work. By custom—except from 1928 through 1931—the next season's models were introduced in connection with the Labor Day holiday on the first Monday in September. As indicated in the December 3, 1930, letter from Hosley to du Pont, the 1931 models were late-arrivers. In fact, the (unofficial) 1930 models were produced until announcement of the (unofficial) 1931 models in March 1931.

The major functional change for the 1931 Series 101 Scouts and Chiefs was a throttle-controlled oil pump. This was still a total-loss oil system, meaning that oil was pumped to the crankcase but not returned. The oil was simply burned up. The new feature was a variable delivery rate based on the amount of throttle opening as well as engine speed. The paint on all 1931 Indians was DuPont Duco lacquer, which proved unpopular because it would not withstand vigorous polishing.

A new Indian-face horn was mounted below the headlight. The chromium-plated embossed headlight rim mentioned earlier, a running change through mid-1930 models, was officially introduced on the 1931 models. The handlebars were reinforced by a crossbar. On the tanks were new transfers, with smaller Indian script and the model name placed beneath the script. For the first time, sales literature clearly indicated that contrasting-color tank panels were available on all models instead of only on the Scout. However, the author believes these panels had been available on 1929 and 1930 Chiefs. On the Scout, aluminum pistons became standard equipment and cast-iron pistons became optional.

On the Four, new lighter, quieter, and smoother running "special alloy" pistons were used with less clearance than earlier aluminum pistons. The new pistons featured oil rings with two slots, and were intended to reduce oil consumption. In the Four clutch, a nine-disc setup replaced the seven-disc setup.

On the Chief, new and heavier right and left flywheel assemblies were fitted to improve smoothness. Earlier flywheels had two large balancing holes, giving the flywheels almost the shape of a wheel with two spokes. The new flywheels had one much smaller balancing hole, opposite the crankpin mounting hole, giving the flywheels a "nearly solid" look. The Chief was also the recipient of new lighter "special alloy" pistons, a la the Four. The motor balance factor was new because of the combination of heavier flywheels and lighter pistons.

These Chief changes were intended to satisfy dealer complaints that the Chief was not as fast, smooth, or reliable as the Harley-Davidson 74. Worse, even Indian's own 45-ci 101 Scout was faster than the Chief! The fastest 101 Scouts were those with the high-performance "B" motors. Special Scout "B"-motor cylinders and heads were listed in *Contact Points* No. 429, June 5, 1931.

1930 ex-Tom Paradise factory hillclimber. *The 45ci engine ran on special fuel with a compression ratio of about 15:1. Output probably exceeded 45 horsepower. Accounts vary, and one story is that Indian built 26 of these engines in 1926. Another version has it that Indian built 20 of them between 1925 and 1930. Several of these Charles Franklin-designed motors were used in board-track races and at least one was outfitted with brakes for road racing. Owner, R. L. Jones.* Mark Mitchell; assistance by Indian Motorcycle Illustrated

Besides standardizing frames, Indian probably had another reason for canceling the Series 101: selling price. Scouts were expensive to build because of their helical gear primary drive and cast-aluminum oil-bath primary case. Harley-Davidson had gotten around a similar cost problem with its 45 twin by adding a small surcharge to its popular big twins in order to subsidize the smaller machine. Unfortunately, such a solution wouldn't work for Indian, as the Four was already very expensive but not a big seller and the Chief was little or perhaps no more popular than the Series 101.

The Four fenders and tanks were made as similar as possible to those of the Chief and Scout, and a set of completely new front forks was used on the three machines. The new front end was wider with a wider leaf spring and taller via longer front forks. The fork connector links were reinforced and had a more pronounced "zig-zag" to clear the new wider front fender. The fork bell cranks had a new shape, and a fork lock was fitted.

These cylinders were not listed in any subsequent parts books, although they may have continued to be available. Inside the "B"-motor heads were special inlet and exhaust valve springs, the same as used on 1922–1925 Chiefs (these parts would be used through 1934). The Scout "B"-motor carburetor was used on the 1931 Chiefs (and continued on 1932 Chiefs). As with the cylinders, the "B" Scout's carburetor manifold and manifold cone were not listed in any subsequent parts books. Giving some clue as to the "B" manifold's design was the manifold gasket, which was used on 1935 and 1936 45-ci "Y" Scout motors, 1937–1942 45-ci Scout motors (all were "Y"), and on 1932–1953 Chiefs. In short, the "B"-Scout manifold was Chief-size.

1932

The Indian range was changed drastically for 1932. Gone was the Series 101 Scout so beloved by dealers and experienced riders. In its place was the Model 203 Scout, which was simply a Scout motor in a Chief frame. The new Scout didn't have the delightful handling of the Series 101, and many dealers were disgusted.

Overall, the biggest change in the 1932 range was the "new look," now influenced by British and European trends. The frame was topped by a pair of "saddle" tanks that enclosed the top frame tube. The tanks in concert with the taller front end had the effect of seating the rider "inside" the motorcycle. The unpopular lacquer finish of 1931 was replaced by DuPont DuLux enamel.

Experience over the years had shown the earlier Four frames were less likely to bend in the event of an accident, as compared to the earlier Scout and Chief frames. This was determined to be due to the widely splayed twin front down tubes on the Fours, whereas the earlier Scout and Chief frames had the two front down tubes joined about halfway up toward the steering head. Therefore, the new 1932 Scout and Chief frame featured widely splayed twin front down tubes that angled in as they continued upward, but didn't join until reaching the steering head.

Although the splayed front down tubes weren't a new Four feature, the Four also featured a new frame. The Scout/Chief frame and the Four frame

Hill Climbs

Hillclimbs grew in popularity in the 1930s until they were perhaps more popular than race meets. Typical hills were sloped about 45 degrees and were 300 or more feet in length. The most widely publicized climbs were those in San Juan Capistrano, California, and Muskegon, Michigan, where national meets were held, but dozens of other locales drew several thousand spectators to each of several seasonal hillclimbs.

All three American factories (Indian, Harley-Davidson, and Excelsior/Henderson) built special hillclimb-

Fred Marwick fights his Indian to the hilltop, circa 1931.

ing motorcycles with overhead-valve engines sporting two exhaust ports per head (engineers were then concentrating on efficient exhaust systems rather than inlet breathing). Forks and frames scarcely resembled standard components. Part of the hillclimb attraction may have been the big V-twins, as American motorcycle racing had become dominated by single-cylinder derivatives of the Indian Prince and the Harley-Davidson Peashooter. With the advent of so-called Class C (stock) racing, 45-ci V-twins again took over the race tracks. Flat-tracking gradually grew in popularity, eventually regaining its favored status by the end of the decade.

1931 series 101 Scout. *Improvements for the 1931 Indians included: cadmium-plated and heavier spokes, Indian face horn, center-mounted headlight, handlebar crossbar, new tank transfers, optional contrasting color tank panel, throttle-controlled oil pump, new muffler, armored taillight wire, and internally expanding rear brake. From a 1930 sales brochure: "Do far horizons beckon? Kick the motor over; give it the gas. Your Indian will take you there speedily, comfortably, economically."* Charles Moore

featured forgings (or castings) that joined the front down tubes and lower tubes. Previously, only the Four had this feature, while earlier twins had the front down tubes curving back in a continuous line to become the lower tubes. Another new feature on the Scout/Chief frame was the mounting provision for the clutch pedal; earlier Scout and Chief models had the clutch mounted to the primary-drive cover.

A drawback of the "new look" layout was increased weight. Longer frame forks and frame tubes meant increased torsional and bending stresses on these components, which was overcome by heavier tubing and forgings. For example, the all-up weight of the Four grew from 451 pounds in 1931 to 495 pounds in 1932. Fortunately, American riders weren't weight conscious.

On the Chief, the standard kickstarter location was the right side. The starter crank could be placed on the left if preferred for sidecar use. For the

first time since 1908, battery ignition was standard on the Scout and Chief, and magneto ignition became optional. The new standard battery ignition operated on the wasted-spark principle, with both cylinder plugs firing on every motor revolution, and included a circuit-breaker mechanism mounted forward of the crankcase. This system dispensed with the need for a distributor, but required extra battery power. Harley-Davidson had used the wasted-spark principle for many years. The Chief's Auto-lite generator was mounted behind the rear cylinder instead of ahead of the front cylinder. This was identical to the Scout, which had earlier had the rear-mounted generator. In the spring of 1932, Indian returned to the utility market they had abandoned at the end of 1928, when the Prince 21-ci single had been terminated. The new low-cost Scout Pony 30.50-ci twin was in a sense a two-cylinder Prince. Many of the Scout Pony components were inherited from the Prince, including the primary drive, clutch, transmission, and kickstarter mechanism. Styling was brought up to date with a teardrop-shaped pair of fuel/oil tanks that hid the upper frame tube. The Scout Pony weighed in at about 330 pounds compared to the old Prince at 271 pounds.

Some design features of the Scout Pony continued throughout the little twin's production life (1932–1941), although there were detail changes over the years. The front fork was a girder design with a central coil spring. Indian termed the frame a "keystone" type because the engine/transmission unit was a load bearing combination that filled the gap between the front

1932 Four. *The 1932 season saw the reinstatement of the annual models policy that had been abandoned from 1928 through 1931. Functionally, there were no major changes in the 1932 Four. Marvin Enochs.*

and rear frame sections. In Britain and Europe this layout had been popular for several years.

The Scout Pony engine was basically a double-up of the former Prince single. Lubrication was total-loss (non-recirculating) as on the Scout and Chief, but there was no tank-mounted hand pump. Ignition was by the wasted-spark principle, with a circuit breaker mounted on the right crankcase and driven by the rear camshaft.

The Scout Pony primary drive was accomplished through a double-row chain, and the drive was protected by a stamped sheet-metal cover. The clutch was a dry Harley-style unit. The left-side kickstarter featured an exposed geared sector integral with the starter arm. These major features were all inherited from the defunct Prince, and their carryover probably helped to hold down manufacturing costs. Scout Pony sales were disappointing, though the fault lay with the terrible economy, not shortcomings in the model.

1933: A Sinking Indian

Despite improvements in management and motorcycle design, by 1933 the company was down to operating at only 5 percent of plant capacity. In February, the accounting department notified general manager Hosley that the company wouldn't be able to meet its next payroll, forcing Hosley to obtain a $10,000 loan. The office force was put on two-thirds time and the factory was closed for one week (without pay to employees). A series of

additional pay cuts and layoffs ensured that there would be enough money to pay those employees still on board.

Among those laid off was Charles Gustafson, Jr., who had been part of the Indian racing department since the Oscar Hedstrom days. Gustafson and his father had also been instrumental in converting Indian road models from F-head to side-valve configuration. DuPont considered filing for bankruptcy, then dropped the idea in favor of financial reorganization. Annual production dropped to 1,667 machines, which was the all-time lowest since production moved to the Wigwam in 1905. During this same period, Harley-Davidson built and sold 3,703 machines, its all-time lowest since its pioneer years.

Despite such traumas, Indian managed to introduce two major changes for the 1933 lineup: the new Motoplane model and dry-sump (recirculating) lubrication on the twins. The Motoplane was a 45-ci version of the Scout Pony. Other than the engine size and the name Motoplane on the tanks, the new model was identical to the Scout Pony. Though this looked good on paper, it proved a problem because of the additional power of the 45-ci motor. There were instances of frame-tube breakage beneath the saddle. In fact, the Motoplane may have been intended from the outset as a stopgap model, because it was around only for the 1933 season.

1932 Four. *For 1932, Indian introduced a new look featuring longer forks and frames that were taller in the front. Saddle height seemed much lower and the rider almost got the feeling of sitting in the motorcycle. A new front fender and new streamlined tanks completed the styling makeover. All models were finished in Du Pont DuLux enamel, as the Duco lacquer finish of 1931 proved unpopular. Marvin Enochs*

1933 Chief. *Dry-sump circulating lubrication debuted on the 1932 twins. Supply and return oil lines are shown in this photo. This example has the standard Harley-style "wasted spark" battery ignition system (there was no distributor, so both cylinders fired on every engine revolution). From 1933 through 1935, the spark-supplying circuit breaker was located on the right side of the motor near the rear exhaust pipe, under a cylindrical cap about the size of a spray-paint-can lid.*

The dry-sump oiling on the twins proved to be a tough engineering problem to solve. During 1933 and 1934 three different oil-pump-drive worm gears were tried, all driven by the front camshaft. Also, different combinations of pumping pistons, and sump (suction, or return) valves were used. Finally, after periods of over-oiling and under-oiling, the dry-sump design was stabilized.

Scouts, Chiefs, and Fours shared a fork change as well. This was the new front brake anchor formed by a lever instead of a telescoping tube.

Atop the fork of each model was a new headlight with a different rim and an adjustable convex lens. On battery-ignition models, the circuit breaker was relocated to the cam case cover on the right side of the crankcase.

Another appearance change was the black cylinders and cylinder heads on all models. The black cylinders and heads probably were brought out as a running change on late-1932 models.

Prior to 1933, customers could order special plating only on individual items. For 1933, Indian offered an optional chromium-plating package

64

that included the items most frequently requested by customers (such as cadmium-plated rims). The special plating package was a convenience to the factory as well as a cost savings for the customers, and buyers could still order special plating on other items not included in the special package if they so desired. Indian used the special plating option throughout the 1930s, though not always explaining the option in publicity releases.

The Great Depression: Dark Age of Motorcycle Sport

Because of the depth of the Great Depression, motorcycle sport reached a low point in the early 1930s. During this period both Indian and Harley-Davidson

1933 Chief. *Black cylinders and cylinder heads introduced in mid-1932 were used throughout 1933 and 1934. Only 1,667 Indians were made in the 1933 business year (October 1932 through September 1933), mostly 1933 models, the lowest total production since 1905. The 1933 models are among the rarest on the contemporary scene. Over the years, most of the few surviving battery-ignition 1932–1935 models were converted to either 1936-style distributor ignition or to magneto ignition. Consequently, this example is extremely rare. Restoration by owner John Rank.*

Indian's racing interest was at an all-time low.

To cope with the harsh economic times, Indian and Harley-Davidson got together in 1933 and invented Class C racing. As the name implies, there already were Classes A and B racing. Class A racing was fully professional, permitting factory-salaried riders, special motorcycles (such as the Franklin-designed 45-ci overhead-valve jobs), and special fuels. Class B was a hybrid class that permitted some special machines to be ridden by nonprofessional riders.

Class C was intended to put racing in the hands of true amateurs using box-stock motorcycles. The principal mechanism used to ensure the stock requirement, was a provision that at least 25 identical motorcycles had to be produced by the manufacturer. With the twin aims of minimizing racing expense and discouraging racing development, compression ratios were limited and fuel had to be ordinary pump gasoline. To further discourage factory and dealer involvement that would ruin this Olympian ideal, riders were required to own their motorcycles and to ride them to the race events. Cubic-inch capacity was limited to 45 for side-valve machines and 30.50 for overhead-valve machines. The latter category was almost an afterthought because only foreign firms were then manufacturing 30-ci overheads, and foreign motorcycles were essentially nonexistent in the United States.

In addition to flat track racing and road racing, which used the mixed-bag rule of 45-ci side-valves versus 30.50-ci overheads, there were provisions for competing on larger stock motorcycles. Machines up to 80 ci (1300 cc) were permitted in hillclimbs and TT races.

Classes A and B continued to run, but top-flight competition was limited to a few riders across the nation who had been entrenched in the system for several years. Class C, then, was probably considered experimental at this point, ready to prove its worth by saving scarce factory and dealer dollars, or ready to quietly expire.

showed increased interest in hillclimbing. The Super-X victories of Joe Petrali and Gene Rhyne had produced much good publicity for Excelsior/Henderson, and Springfield was naturally in a mood to reap some of the same rewards. When the Super-X and Henderson marques folded in March 1931, Indian managed to hire Gene Rhyne, the 1930 National Hillclimb Champion, for the 1931 season. Rhyne joined Indian's top established slant artist, Orie Steele, who had been winning big climbs for a decade. Also on the Indian hillclimbing team was young Howard Mitzell, who was to remain a top hillclimber on Indians into the 1960s.

Flat-track racing was a dying sport, as the harsh economic times and the dissimilarity between 21.35-ci one-cylinder racers and larger V-twin motorcycles combined to kill spectator appeal.

Indian suffered a great loss in October 1932 when engineer Charles B. Franklin died at the age of 46. As the man behind the most successful of the eight-valves, the surprisingly fast side-valves, and the later overhead-valve racers, his death was a blow to revival of Indian racing glory.

By 1933, racing had been reduced to a local amateur exercise. Many races were "outlaw" events, that is, unsanctioned. It was also at about this time that the European style of speedway racing became popular, and as the most successful of the speedway bikes were English-built JAPs or Rudges,

Classic Styling, Classic Racing

1934–1939

Beginning with one mid-season 1934 model, Indian ushered in a new era of classic open-fender styling. Announced in February 1934, the Sport Scout was graced with beautifully curved and flared fenders, plus a war-bonnet-clad Indian head and Indian script on each tank. DuPont's family connections enabled Indian to buy paint cheaply, which resulted in an explosion of color options. The "color war" with Harley-Davidson reached its zenith in 1934, when Indian offered twenty-four *standard* one- and two-color options, plus an extra-cost option of *any* nonlisted colors available in DuPont paints.

The Sport Scout, like the Scout Pony, used a keystone frame in which the motor acted as a stressed member. In fact, both the Sport Scout and the Scout Pony had no frame tubing joining the front down tube and the rear fork; all the space was filled by the engine/transmission package, which was bolted to front and rear mounting plates that were, in turn, bolted to the frame.

In theory, the Sport Scout combined the weight-saving construction of the Prince-Pony-Motoplane layout with the rigidity of the semi-unit construction, now-defunct Series 101. The Scout-Prince-Pony-Motoplane layout had an entirely separate engine and transmission. The Sport Scout had the engine and transmission bolted together (although they were separated by plates). This allowed the primary chain to be tightened by an internal shoe, thus doing away with the need to relocate the gearbox and consequently the need to tighten the rear chain as well. The reason for qualifying the keystone setup as better "in theory" is that little if any weight was saved despite the appearance of light weight. The old Series 101 Scout had weighed 370 pounds according to factory specifications; the new Sport Scout weighed 385 pounds according to the factory specifications.

Indian and Harley-Davidson used different approaches to side-valve cylinder design. Based on gas flow experiments conducted with the cooperation of the Massachusetts Institute of Technology (M.I.T.), Indian kept the Sport Scout's valves as close to the cylinder bore as possible, which improved gas flow. Harley-Davidson, which had jumped into the side-valve game with the 1929 season, used an approach pioneered by the Excelsior company. This consisted of leaving enough room between the valves and the cylinder bore to provide a cooling air space between the valve pocket and the cylinder proper. However, in later years, the evolutionary path of Harley-Davidson racing development vindicated Indian's findings and brought the valves ever closer to the bore.

Optional aluminum cylinder heads were offered for the Scout, Chief, and Sport Scout. These were shaped the same as the standard iron heads. Like

1937 Four. Reported Indian News *November-December 1936, "For those who prefer quietness, smoothness and comfort—the Indian 4 is the machine. Idles along smoothly in high gear at low speeds and accelerates quietly and evenly to a fast cruising speed that over long stretches will outdistance the average machine. The new refinements and improvements make this the 'Luxury' motorcycle of the year." Owner: Rudy Litke.* Jeff Hackett; assistance by *Indian Motorcycle Illustrated*

1937 Four. *For 1937, Four carburetion was changed from a single Marvel carburetor to dual Zenith carburetors. Owner: Rudy Litke.* Jeff Hackett; assistance by *Indian Motorcycle Illustrated*

the Sport Scout, the Scout and Chief had new chain-driven primary drives.

Production for 1934 totaled 2,809 machines. Harley-Davidson built 9,000–10,000 for the comparable 12-month period prior to extending their 1934 sales season by six months.

On the competition front, the Class C category invented the year before actually got off the ground in 1934. Because Class C had yet to prove itself, there was not yet a circuit of individual flat-track championships as there was for Class A jobs. The only Class C national title races held in 1934

were a 200-mile National TT Championship and a 6-hour National Championship race; both events fell to Harley-Davidson riders.

1935: Grace Multiplied

For 1935, the Chief, Scout, and Four were treated to the graceful fenders and tank trim introduced on the 1934 Sport Scout. This was the last year in which Indian enjoyed a clear styling advantage over Harley-Davidson—bearing in mind that the later skirted fenders were controversial in their time. A 1935 Chief's classic lines are all the better when parked next to a 1935 Harley. Indians had teardrop-shaped tanks, while Harleys had sort of rounded-off trapezoid (humped-back) tanks. Making matters worse, Harley-Davidson put little screws down the middle of its tank. The Indian fenders and chain guard also had a styling flair not found on Harleys.

Beginning in 1935, Indian offered three optional paint schemes for the tanks. In fact, Indian not only offered more standard color choices than Harley, but for $5.00 extra would supply any color available from DuPont.

Nickel-plated cylinders and cylinder heads were standard on all models, whether equipped with standard or "Y" motors.

1934 Chief. *Rider's-eye view of a 1934 Chief shows an internally illuminated speedometer, a first for 1934. Speedometers came in several types, including 80- and 100-mile-per-hour faces, lighted and unlighted, and with or without a maximum-speed indicator. In this photograph, the maximum-speed hand is registering about 85 miles per hour. One button resets the maximum-speed hand to zero, and another button zeroes the trip meter. Restoration by owner Dave Halliday.*

A styling point in Harley-Davidson's favor was its front fork, which was simple and elegant compared to Indian's leaf-spring fork. Only Indian lovers can find beauty in the leaf-spring fork.

A technical comparison to a contemporary Harley-Davidson reveals several points in Indian's favor. Indian offered a four-speed transmission to Harley's three. Indian had dry-sump (recirculating) lubrication while Harley still ran total-loss. Indian had reversible throttle and gearshift lever locations and reversible clutch-pedal action; Harley didn't. Indian had a cast-aluminum oil-bath primary-chain case, while Harley used a leaky, pressed-steel chaincase. Indian offered optional magneto ignition; Harley offered only battery ignition. Indian built a lightweight twin and a four; Harley, neither.

In 15 years of side-valve motorcycle competition, Indian had set numerous speed records. Harley had six years of side-valve V-twin experience but no speed records for the side-valve engines. The 1935 Scout, Sport Scout, and Chief were available from midseason with optional larger "Y" cylinders and matching aluminum cylinder heads (somewhat confusingly, the "Y" manifold, "Y" cylinders, and "Y" cylinder heads were not featured in company sales literature until 1936). The cylinders of the Scout and Sport Scout had new inlet ports that were angled about 30 degrees toward the Y-shaped inlet manifold; Chief cylinders didn't have the Y-shaped manifold and companion cylinder porting despite the "Y" motor term. In modern lingo, the new "Y"

heads had a pent roof—in cross section the area between the valve pocket and the bore was like an inverted "V." These so-called "trench" heads provided much improved low- to mid-range torque. Feature by feature, the 1935 Indian lineup had it all over Harley-Davidson and soon made this apparent on the race track.

Indian began to make itself known in 1935 Class C racing and record-setting. In February, Rody Rodenburg rode a Sport Scout to victory in the Jacksonville, Florida, 200-mile road race, the forerunner of the Daytona 200. In May, an unusual record was set by brothers Steve and Roger Whiting. Alternating in the saddle of their solo (no sidecar) Chief, they set a new transcontinental record of 4 days, 20 hours, 36 minutes. Another Class C record was accomplished in May on California's Muroc Dry Lake when a Chief rolled 100 miles in 1 hour, 17 minutes, and 48 seconds. At Langhorne, Pennsylvania, "Woodsie" Castonguay won the 100-mile Class C national in September on a Sport Scout. Other Indians took second, third, fifth, sixth, and seventh.

Comparison of Indian and Harley-Davidson Factories

In 1935, the Indian plant was perhaps more efficient than the Harley-Davidson plant. Harley-Davidson board member William H. Davidson reported the following to the Harley board in July 1935:

The Indian factory is rather unique in that they are operating with a crew far smaller than ours, yet appear to be doing a good job. Their office force, to my observation was about one-third the size of ours. . .

Their engineering department consists of about six men, including the Drafting Department. Their experimental room was manned by three persons. Despite the small organization, they have just completed development on a brand new four-cylinder machine which has just gone into production. They have also just redesigned their large Traffic Car and apparently they have licked all of their major troubles with the Sport 45 and their Big Chief.

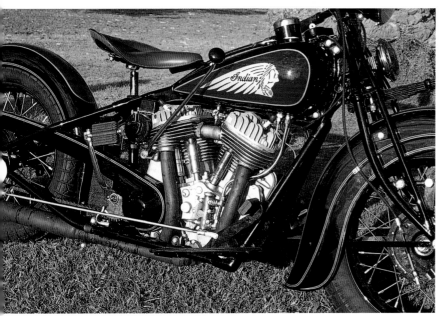

1935 Chief. *Following the lead of the new mid-1934 45-ci Sport Scout, the 1935 Chief and Four were fitted with swooping, valanced front and rear fenders. This motorcycle has the standard tank panel, but two other tank panels were offered as same-price options beginning in 1935, these being the "Arrow" and "V" panels. New extra-cost options included "Y" cylinders and "Y" aluminum heads as shown on this example. Nickel plating of cylinders and heads returned on both "Y" and standard motors. Magneto ignition was optional, at extra cost, in lieu of wasted-spark ignition. Restoration by Jim Parker; owner: Peter Arundel.*

1936 Chief. *This "Y"-motor 1936 Chief has been restored with 1935 tanks featuring the small, screw-on filler caps. The "V" tank panel is used. New for 1936 were the "T" oil lines that fed the inlet and exhaust valve guides. The January–February 1936* Indian News *noted, "The Indian 74, the 'Y' motored Chief—more so than in 1935—will be the hard rider's pet during 1936. The smallest lubrication details have been attended . . . trouble free . . . once again the hard rider's motorcycle." Restoration by Bollenbach Engineering.*

1936 Chief. *This restoration features the correct period saddlebags. There were two schools of thought on customizing bikes in the 1930s. One approach was to cut down the fenders and remove accessories. The other was to bolt on more accessories. Dealers preferred the latter approach because this meant extra income from the higher profit margin bolt-ons offered. Restoration by Bollenbach Engineering.*

1936 Chief. *Optional, extra-cost "Y" motors had newly shaped cylinder heads of the "trench" design. "Y"-motor cylinder heads and cylinders had deeper finning. The streamlined "bug strainer" air horn was first cataloged on the 1936 models, but may have been phased in on late-1935 models. Earlier air horns were circular. The primary-drive system was changed from helical gears to four-row chain in 1934, and the primary-drive case and cover were reshaped.*
Restoration by Bollenbach Engineering.

Early-1936 Four. *In the middle of the 1935 season Indian introduced the so-called "upside-down" Four, which featured a reversal of the valve configuration. The exhaust valves were now on top, and the inlet valves were on the bottom. Higher power output was claimed, but the appearance drove away prospective buyers.*

The Indian factory carries a very limited inventory as they try as far as possible to make up just what they need from day to day. They do not build up motors or enameled parts for stock as we do. . .

In going through their factory, it is rather difficult to determine whether they are operating on a solid, highly efficient basis, or whether they are merely going along in the hope of making a success without any practical plan.

In December, Indian common stock was valued at $2.50. Back in 1930, when E. Paul du Pont had bought into Indian, the stock was valued at $11.75. Annual production for 1935 totaled 3,715 machines. Harley-Davidson built approximately 11,000 in that same period.

1936: The Ugly Duckling

Indian made a bad product decision by bringing out the 1936 "upside-down" Four during the middle of the 1935 sales season. The problem was

the ugly duckling appearance caused by having the inlet valves and carburetor down on the side, and the exhaust valves on top, thus the nickname "upside-down."

The idea was to get the hotter exhaust valves in closer proximity to the cylinder head, which would aid heat dissipation due to the large head area. Also, heat loss was enhanced by changing the head cooling fins to a sunburst configuration. The improved exhaust-heat dissipation did away with the old theory of having the relatively cool inlet gas flow from above and therefore assist in cooling the area below that surrounded the exhaust valve. With the inlet gasses now coming in from the relatively cooler side location, and with the exhaust valve heat better dissipated, there was less reduction in inlet-gas mass flow due to overheating the inlet charge. The result was increased power, although the amount of power improvement was never made public.

continued on page 75

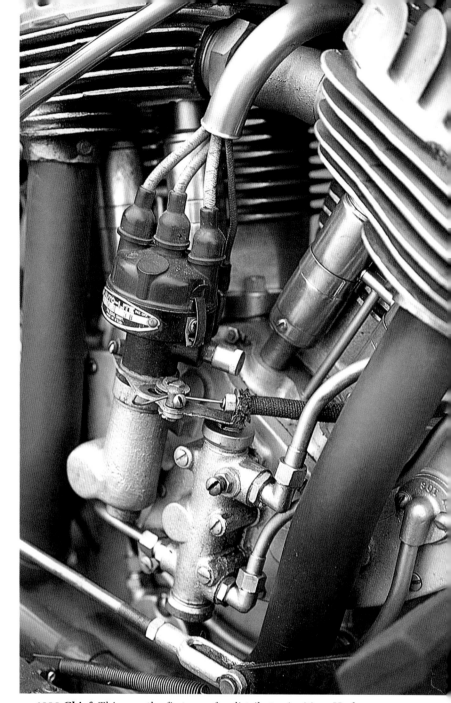

1936 Chief. *This was the first year for distributor ignition. Harley-Davidson continued to claim their wastcd-spark battery ignition was more reliable because it didn't have a distributor. Wrong! The brown distributor cap is correct; it was used on new battery ignition Indians from 1936 through 1953. Restoration by Bollenbach Engineering.*

1936 Chief. *Again we see the "V" tank panel, this time on a standard-motor 1936 Chief. Standard pinstriping was in gold, but special striping colors could be ordered, as shown here. Restoration by Jim Parker, assistance by Warwick Ellis; owner: Peter Arundel.*

Ed Kretz

Inside every motorcyclist, whatever the age, is a kid. The little boy side of their personalities took over Ed Kretz and his buddy Harrison Reno on the night before the biggest motorcycle race in the nation. Kretz and Reno, with their race-ready Sport Scouts, took on all comers in a series of drag races up and down Daytona Beach. It never occurred to them that they were robbing from the next day's performance.

With Sunday morning hangovers, Kretz and Reno headed for the beach. The race course was 3.2 miles long consisting of two straights about 1-1/2 miles each connected by two turns heavily bermed with sand. The race date and starting time were predicated on the tides, as it was essential to have firm sand, yet avoid the water during the north run up the beach. The back half of the

1937, Ed "Ironman" Kretz wins the first Daytona 200.

1937, Kretz with Daytona trophy.

course, an asphalt road, was deceiving to spectators. There were gentle-looking ripples in the tar, but the speed of the motorcycles, together with their rigid frames and limited front-fork travel, made for very rough riding. Tires took their leave of terra firma, as the rigid-framed motorcycles leaped 10 to 15 feet forward on the rougher bumps. Riders actually lost contact with their bikes, save for the handlegrips and tiptoes on the pegs or footboards.

Eighty-six riders started, five abreast, at 10-second intervals. Kretz was two rows back, but that made no difference, as each rider was billed only for the time elapsed since his official start.

Just after the finish of the second lap, Kretz overtook front runners Lester Hillbish on a Sport Scout and E. Miller on a Norton single. This meant Kretz was actually more than 20 seconds ahead after two laps. He added to his lead with every lap. Kretz spilled twice. Each time he jerked the 350-pound motorcycle up as though it were a bicycle, and he was off and running in seconds. In fact, stop watches showed his second spill had cost him only six seconds compared to his average lap times.

Kretz won the race, his second consecutive 200-mile title. Harrison Reno paid the price of the night before, his Sport Scout expiring at 150 miles while he was in third place. Writing for *The Motorcyclist*, journalist Chet Billings referred to Kretz's "iron man" stamina throughout the race, and ever afterwards writers leaped to this term in trying to describe Ed Kretz's style.

continued from page 71

Unfortunately, the exhaust-over-inlet design was unattractive. The upside-down Fours were sales disasters that lingered one more year with minor improvements. With the worst sort of timing for Indian, Harley-Davidson launched their 61-ci overhead-valve twin in 1936, which became a sales leader and long-run hit. As if to prove the point that the 1936 Four wasn't fully engineered, there were four different versions of carburetor hookups during the year.

Elsewhere in the lineup, the Scout was renamed the Standard Scout to clarify the distinction between this model and the Sport Scout. The Standard Scout, Chief,

Early-1936 Four. *This example has the standard tank panel. Chinese Red was a popular color promoted by Indian from 1931 through 1939. This finish of black and Chinese Red was available as an extra-cost option to 1936 customers, as was any color available in DuPont enamel. Owner: Berland Sullivan.*

and Sport Scout were equipped with "T" oil lines that fed the valve guides. This was a good idea because the earlier Indian system of relying on crankcase pressure alone was only marginally effective. Earlier motors tended to either over-oil or under-oil the valve guides depending on the riders' breather system setup. Indian dealer and speed record setter Rollie Free called the earlier layout the "run in rust" system because, generally, not enough oil was sucked up through the valve guides. Unfortunately, the "T" lines were a bad idea with respect to oil leakage. The problem was sealing off the area between the valve-spring covers and the "T" lines.

Distributor battery ignition was standard, replacing the 1932–1934 standard of wasted-spark ignition. For the first time, the stoplight switch was provided as standard equipment. To accommodate the new standard-equipment stoplight switch, a boss was added to the frame of each model. Incidentally, the year 1936 saw the largest amount of changes in small parts (such as clips and brackets) that was to occur during the era of E. Paul du Pont (1930–1945). This suggests an intensive engineering program.

Production totaled 5,028 machines to Harley-Davidson's 11,000.

Racing: The Sport Scout Hits Its Stride

In January, Ed Kretz won the 200-mile Class C National Championship at Savannah, Georgia, at an average speed of 70.03 miles per hour. Fred Ludlow reached the almost unbelievable speed of 128.57 miles per hour on a Sport Scout during a speed meet in April at Muroc Dry Lake.

Admittedly, this wasn't a Class C mark because Ludlow used special fuel and made the speed runs in one direction only, which permitted the assistance of a very strong tail wind.

Lester Hillbish won the Langhorne, Pennsylvania, 100-mile National at a record 81.06 miles per hour, and six of the first 10 finishers rode Indians. In preparing for the race, Howard Mitzell made an interesting discovery. By eliminating the characteristic heart shape of the internal side of the cylinder head between the valves, Mitzell was able to improve breathing to a degree that more than compensated for the resulting lower compression ratio. This approach was to be the cornerstone of subsequent side-valve racing development for the next 30 years.

Two transcontinental records also fell to Indian that year. In June, Rody Rodenburg crossed the continent on a Sport Scout in 71 hours and 20 minutes, despite getting off course and riding an extra 300 miles. However, his long-time associate and former boss, Rollie Free, told the author that Rodenburg and a friend actually used a car and towed the Sport Scout across the continent. "Too bad," said Free, "they could have made some real money by claiming that time as the automobile record!" In any event, Rodenburg's time was the acknowledged motorcycle record until 1959. In September, L. C. Smith rode a sidecar outfit minus a codriver and crossed the nation in 86 hours and 55 minutes, breaking the 1935 Harley-Davidson sidecar record of Earl and Dot Robinson. At Syracuse, New York, Fred Toscani won the 25-mile Class A National on a 21.35-ci single, one of the last Indian wins in this dying branch of the sport.

In October, reacting to the highly publicized successes of the Sport Scout, Harley-Davidson board member William H. Davidson (Willy G.'s father) reported to the Harley board that the Sport Scout ". . . seems to be a better job than ours."

1937

The most visible change to the 1937 lineup was the relocation of the gearshift lever to the forward tank area. On the Standard Scout and the Chief,

the original Laconia National, a 200-miler that was termed a TT. This event was so physically demanding that Ed earned the nickname "Iron Man," which stuck with him the rest of his career.

Indian Dominates Racing on the Track and the Street

Since 1926, Indian had reigned as the fastest American motorcycle because of Johnny Seymoure's 132-mile-per-hour run. Harley-Davidson took this honor away in early 1937 by setting an American (unrestricted, Class A) record at Daytona Beach, running 136.183 miles per hour.

In other racing, however, Indian remained dominant, with several Sport Scout riders joining Ed Kretz to ensure Indian's supremacy in 1937. At races in Reading, Pennsylvania, and Richmond, Virginia, Lester Hillbish set new 5-mile records. Hillbish also won the 100-mile TT championship at Old Orchard, Maine, and the 25-mile flat-track championship at Springfield, Illinois. The latter win rewarded him with the number-one plate until the next

this change introduced linkages between the lever and the transmission, whereas previously these models benefited from the delightful direct-action relationship between the lever and the transmission. On the other models, which previously had an indirect shift setup with intermediary linkages, the new forward shift-lever location increased the shifting sloppiness. The forward gearshift lever was apparently necessary from a styling standpoint, a triumph of looks over function. Still, it could be argued that this was an improvement for two-up riding because the old "jockey style" lever was difficult to use when the rider moved forward to accommodate the passenger.

All 45-ci and 74-ci twins were now fitted with "Y" motors. The little twin previously known as the Scout Pony, was renamed Junior Scout.

On the Four only, the carburetors were changed—two Zenith units were used. On the Sport Scout, the front fender valance was increased so that the fender became identically shaped to that of the Standard Scout, Chief, and Four.

On the nation's race tracks, the man of the hour was Ed Kretz. Kretz won the inaugural Daytona 200 on the beach in January 1937 and led each of the next four prewar 200-milers before dropping out. He won two consecutive 100-mile nationals on the Langhorne, Pennsylvania, mile-long dirt oval in 1937 and 1938, and again won in 1940. In 1938, Kretz copped

1937 Chief. *This 1937 Chief shows off popular accessories. The forward-mounted gearshift lever was a new feature for 1937. The tandem passenger seat fell into disfavor at about this time because of the new twin-passenger buddy seat. This bike has the optional magneto ignition. Restoration by Bollenbach Engineering.*

1937 Chief. *Larger, half-twist, "bayonet" filler caps debuted on the 1936 models except for the Scout Pony. The two-shade green finish was popular in the 1930s either as a standard color, as listed in 1935, or as an extra-cost option in other years.*

1937 Chief. *When equipped with magneto ignition, the Chief, Scout, and Sport Scout had the distributor drive hole covered with a plate. Behind the front exhaust pipe is the crankcase breather.*

Springfield mile in 1938.

In the summer of 1937, Indianapolis Indian dealer Roland "Rollie" Free won a $100 bet with the owner of the Harley-Davidson 45 that had set a Class C record of 102.047 miles per hour when ridden by Joe Petrali at Daytona Beach the previous January. Free goaded owner and Harley dealer J. B. Jones into a country-road match race against Free's Sport Scout, with some particularly juicy lines. "Look, I came down here on an Indian Scout named *Papoose*, with my wife on back . . . I can beat the Harley beach record with my wife on back of the machine—double!" Instead of putting up the money, Jones offered a gentleman's bet, to which Free scornfully replied, "I never had a gentleman's bet with a Harley guy in my life!" The following spring, Rollie Free would officially back up his mouth with his money by establishing a new 45-ci record for Indian.

Annual production totaled 6,030 machines. Harley-Davidson built 12,100.

1937 Sport Scout. The Sport Scout debuted as a mid-1934 model. Evolutionary changes from 1934 through 1937 dealt mostly with fine tuning the dry-sump (circulating) oiling system and with variations of the crankcase breathing system. The 1937 press releases and catalogs didn't get more specific than "a wide variety of colors," but Chinese Red and silver had been Indian offerings for several years. Restoration by Jerry Cordy.

1937 Sport Scout. Owners could order a black frame at extra cost during this era. The standard-issue frame was color-matched to the sides of the tanks and fenders. The Sport Scout's three-row primary chain ran in a cast-aluminum oil-bath chain case, as did the Chief's four-row chain. The keystone frame had the engine and transmission filling the gap between the front down tube and the rear frame section.

1938

The author has used the term "classic open-fenders era" to describe the 1934 Sport Scout and all large models built from 1935 through 1939. This era came to full flower in 1938 with the addition of a tank-top instrument panel on the Chief, Four, and Sport Scout. Additionally, the 1938-only speedometer and ammeter were lovely gray-faced instruments with red lettering, complimented by a gray ignition switch.

A variety of detail changes were made throughout the model line. The "T" oil lines used on 1936 and 1937 twins were eliminated. On the Chief, new cylinders received different valve guides and larger fins in the exhaust valve area. The Standard Scout was eliminated from the range. Fork shields were added—one type for the Chief and Four fork, and another for the Sport Scout fork. Oddly, the Junior Scout crankcases, transmission case, and transmission case cover were changed from aluminum to iron! All these iron parts were either painted or plated to achieve a light color, but the reasons for the changes are unknown. On the Sport Scout and Chief, the oil-pump assembly differed in having provision for the distributor drive. The new wraparound cam-case cover was machined differently to accommodate the new oil-pump assembly. On the Chief, new alloy pistons of the "T"-slot design were offered. The new rings were aimed at increasing oil mileage. Production for 1938 clocked in at 3,650 machines. Harley-Davidson built 7,658 two-wheeled motorcycles and 519 Servi-Cars.

In retrospect, Indian made a significant mistake in designing their 1938 range: In the absence of much-needed improvements to the Four, Indian would have been better served by spending its limited resources in

The 1930s Shop Scene

Top racing stars such as Ed Kretz could not rely on racing wins for all their income. Ed Kretz and Frank Christian reminisced about working at the Floyd Clymer Indian shop in Los Angeles.

Christian: "The worst thing about working for Clymer was the pay . . ."

Kretz: "Payday was the worst part about working at Clymer's. He used to give me a dollar extra, and . . ."

Christian: "I know exactly what you were going to say—about Slim working on that outboard motor. Slim Shoemaker was working there . . . If we punched in our time cards the entire six days—if we punched in before 8 o'clock, and punched out not until after 6 . . ."

Clymer's Indian shop in Los Angeles. The photo was taken in 1935, but count it for any year up through 1939 because only the motorcycles changed. Notice the three men behind the counter facing the camera. The one in the middle is Morty Graves, former board track star. The one on your right (the counter's left) is Floyd Clymer.

not do that. If I do that, then I'll have to do it for the next guy. That's the rule. You didn't punch the clock on time; no dollar.' That was Clymer, that was him. Yet, he was really not bad to us—not really good—but considering everything, he was not bad."

Kretz: "I used to live in Pomona when I worked there, and I used to go like hell to get there. One day, it was just 8 o'clock, and I jumped out of the car. I'd parked on the other side of the street, and I was going to come back and park my car later. I opened the door real quick, and here a kid came by with his bicycle and hit the door and just went ass over tea kettle. I yelled, 'Just a minute, I'll be right back!' I went in there and punched it, and I was right

Kretz: "We even had to punch out and in for lunch."

Christian: "And if you had a perfect card, at the end of the week, Clymer would give you an extra dollar. So here's Slim, he's working back there on the last day of the week. Some guy came in with an outboard motor. Slim was sitting there eating his lunch. We had a barrel there, to run these outboard motors in. The guy was in a heck of a hurry, so Clymer asked Slim to stick the motor in the barrel and run it. Slim stuck the motor in the barrel and played around with it a few minutes to get it to run, while he was still eating his sandwich. When time to punch the clock came, Slim forgot it. All at once, he thought of it, so he ran up and punched the clock two minutes late. Clymer would not give him that dollar! Clymer said, 'I can

on the nose at 8 o'clock. Then I went back and told the kid that I was sure sorry that he'd hit that door."

Christian: "That's how important that extra dollar was, when you were only getting eighteen a week."

Kretz: "We made three bucks a day. I lived in Pomona and was paying eighteen dollars a month rent. I finally figured out how to work that time clock if I was two or three minutes late getting there. I'd take another time card and put over my card and punch it and get the 8, and then at 9 o'clock I'd cover the 8 and punch it and get the two zeroes!"

Christian: "The best thing about working at Clymer's was working on motorcycles. We loved working on motorcycles!"

converting the Chief to overhead-valve design. Big twins ruled the American market, and a fully updated Chief would have been the basis of a stronger company.

Indian did make several worthwhile improvements to the Four; unfortunately, it wasn't improved enough. A fundamental mistake was the lack of an oil filter and an oil cooler. The provision of these would have more than made up for the challenging cooling requirements posed by an air-cooled, in-line four-cylinder motor. The change to cylinders cast in pairs did improve cooling somewhat but not nearly enough. Surprisingly, development tests proved that putting iron between cylinders number one and two and between three and four aided cooling by conducting the head outward into the air stream. The earlier arrangement of each cylinder cast individually

allowed hot air pockets to develop between the cylinders. Though there is no denying the classic status of the beautiful Four, Indian should have fully updated this design.

A change in the right direction, however, were the 1938 Daytona motors. The October 4, 1937, *Contact Points* No. 472 sets the stage: "For the competition rider or for the rider who demands more powerful motorcycle equipment, the new Daytona motored Sport Scout 45 and Chief 74 motorcycles are available. In Daytona models, the motors are specially tuned and tested to insure maximum performance. Features of this motor include: hand-polished valve ports, high-compression aluminum heads, trunk-type pistons fitted with narrow rings, magneto ignition, clearances to accommodate high-speeds, and in addition, competition spark plugs."

1938:
Eight out of Twelve for Indian

It seemed that Indian Sport Scout racing motorcycles were faster than Harley-Davidson 45 racing motorcycles. The Harleys seemed more reliable, but their reliability edge was more debatable than the Sport Scout's speed margin.

An introduction is in order. Tom Sifton was a famous Harley-Davidson so-called tuner—he was really a scientist in the true sense of the word. From 1938 through 1954, Sifton-prepared Harley racers had 5 or more miles per hour on hand than did the factory-prepared Harleys, and a good 10 miles per hour more speed than the run-of-the-mill Harley privateers. On half-mile dirt tracks, where acceleration was more important than top speed, the Sifton Harleys ran with taller gearing and still accelerated faster than all rivals.

I asked Tom Sifton, "Which were faster, Harleys or Indians?" Of course, I knew I'd asked a silly question, because racing history showed that each brand won its share. But I wanted to hear just how Sifton would lay the issue to rest.

As the headline shows, Indian had the edge in late-1930s dirt-track racing.

Sifton admitted that from late 1951 through 1953, his Harleys were outperformed by the Sport Scouts of Bobby Hill, Bill Tuman, and Ernie Beckman. But that was part of the ebb and flow of racing. Sifton took over again in 1954 and was never equaled.

Sifton's answer, addressing the long-haul history of Indian versus Harley-Davidson:

That is not a good question. I'm talking practically; I'm not talking emotionally. A good tuner—a *builder*, not just a tuner—they keep calling the guys tuners . . . A *builder* to me is a guy who gets in and he changes the balance and the flywheel, or he changes the combustion chamber, or he makes or obtains cams to help him; that, to me, is a builder. Well, a good builder could take either one of them . . . a good man could take an Indian and beat the Harleys, or a good man could take a Harley and beat the Indians. The racing got down pretty much to builders.

In general, these under-publicized high-performance motors, variously known as "B" motors, Savannah motors, Daytona motors, and finally as Bonneville motors, were built with a common philosophy. Their main characteristics of looser clearances, polished internals, careful assembly and balancing, and the inclusion of some special parts were doubtless long-standing practices. On late-1938 Daytona motors, new right and left flywheels were constructed of "Z" metal, a cross between easily machineable iron and durable steel.

Racing

Ed Kretz and the Castonguay brothers were the Indian headliners of 1938. Kretz won his second consecutive Langhorne 100-mile title and the inaugural Laconia event, a 200-mile TT national. Daytona Beach was a disappointment, with the 200-mile title falling to Harley-Davidson rider Ben Campanale. Indian riders retaliated, and by May, held every Class C record for half-mile tracks. Harley-Davidson broke into the half-mile-track record book in June by setting a 5-mile record, but at year's end Indian still owned

eight out of 12 Class C racing records. Woodsie Castonguay set 3- and 10-mile records at Reading, Pennsylvania, and a 25-mile record in winning the Springfield, Illinois, race to finish the 1938 season as the Class C dirt track champion. The Springfield title meant the prestigious number-one plate went to an Indian rider for the second consecutive year. Frenchy Castonguay, Woodsie's brother, won the Topsfield, Massachusetts, 8-mile championship and set a record in the process. In the year-end poll, Ed Kretz was named the nation's most popular rider.

Indians were fast in a straight line as well. On March 17, 1938, at Daytona Beach, Rollie Free captured two new Class C records, hitting 109.65 miles per hour on a fully equipped 74-ci Chief and 111.55 miles per hour on a 45-ci Sport Scout. The Sport Scout record eclipsed Harley-mounted Joe Petrali's 1937 speed of 102.047 by almost 10 miles per hour.

Free's Daytona Class C records were broken in September by Indian rider Fred Ludlow, under the sponsorship of West Coast distributor Hap Alzina and the tuning hands of Red Fenwick. On the salt flats of Bonneville, Ludlow rode a Sport Scout to 115.126 miles per hour and a Chief to

1937 Sport Scout. *The crankcase breather tube exits the cam-case cover and continues to the rear chain. This was the fourth variation of crankcase breathing on the four-year-old Sport Scout, an indication that the factory never solved this problem for any twin-cylinder models.*

120.747 miles per hour. The 1938 Class C record runs by Free and Ludlow solidified Indian's sales dominance of the 45-ci category. However, Harley-Davidson continued to dominate the more lucrative big-twin field.

1939

Indian President E. Paul du Pont visited the New York World's Fair in 1939. While there, he purchased three motorcycles, a Norton single, a BMW, and a Triumph vertical twin. The three motorcycles influenced the design of three forthcoming Indians, the so-called "big-base" Scout, the prototype X-44 four-cylinder, and the production Model 841 shaft-drive machine for the U.S. Army.

The Norton had a built-in crankcase scraper, a setup that company had used for several years. The built-in scraper was a feature Indian adopted for the big-base Sport Scouts. The BMW obviously sparked Indian's interest in shaft-drive motorcycles, and ultimately led to the prototype X-44 and

the Model 841 Army motorcycle. The Triumph layout, with one camshaft on each side of the motor, was favored on the prototype X-44.

A new "World's Fair" tank panel was available on the 1939 models and, in fact, was the standard issue unless an owner specified one of the earlier tank-panel designs. Metallic paint jobs were optional. The Junior Scout was offered in optional Navajo Blue as well as the long-running Indian Red. The Sport Scout featured a "barrel" spring (larger coils in the middle of the spring) in lieu of the standard spring on the front fork. On all models but the Junior Scout, a round air cleaner replaced the former arrow-shaped air horn. Likewise, on all models but the Junior Scout, the rear fender wore a chrome bumper, the same one later used on the skirted-fender models. Optional magneto ignition was reinstated on the 1939 Fours.

The 1935–1938 "Y" trench heads were replaced with non-trench heads that were externally identical except for the subtle difference of no small hump where the trench (or inverted "V") had been. In eliminating the trench

1938 Chief. The small, fold-back seat in the front is for the rider when carrying a passenger on the regular solo saddle. This was called "riding short coupled." From a 1938 advertisement, ". . . truly the most powerful, easiest handling, most comfortable mount ever offered in a stock model. The rider who owns this two-fisted new Indian Chief is king of the road—he is out front to stay."

Right

1938 Chief. The 1938 Fours, Chiefs, and Sport Scouts benefitted from the new tank-top instrument panel. When Indian ran out of the gray ignition switches that were a cataloged feature of the 1938 models, amber or black switches were substituted. Green pinstriping was standard for the maroon and orange finish. The gray gearshift knob was shown in the sales catalogs but, according to factory old-timers, wasn't actually put into production. Owner/restorer Dan Olberg

heads, Indian was bowing to market pressure. By sacrificing better torque in the constantly used low- and mid-rpm ranges, the 1939 heads offered slightly higher maximum speed—always a bigger bragging point among riders.

On the Chief and Sport Scout, the "Z" metal flywheels introduced on late-1938 Daytona motors became standard issue on all models. "Bonneville" motors, the successor to the 1938 Daytona motor, featured new connecting rods. New Chief and Sport Scout cylinder heads featured a larger base which blended in with the cylinder fins. New Chief pistons had a different shape in order to reduce tension on the upper compression rings.

Chief rings were Ferrox treated to prevent cylinder scuffing during break-in. New Chief cams had revised lift profiles for higher maximum power and increased gas flow. Also, new ramps on each cam base decreased valve acceleration and noise. These changes applied to standard and Bonneville motors, although each had their own cams and shafts. Bonneville motors only had new inlet and exhaust lifters.

Annual production totaled 3,012 machines (eight months). Harley-Davidson built 7,695 two-wheeled motorcycles during a 12-month period.

continued on page 87

1938 Chief. *Indian Red and Chinese Red were a standard 1935 combination, and remained on riders' want lists during an era of custom orders. This bike has the extra-cost, optional black frame and fork. Black cylinders are a concession to practicality; the original nickel-plated jugs rust rapidly. The Harley saddle shown is favored by some riders. Restoration by Starklite Cycle.*

1938 Sport Scout. This 1938 Sport Scout was restored with extra-cost options of nonstandard color plus black frame and fork. The windshield is a currently available item. The Antique Motorcycle Club of America doesn't deduct judging points for such a non-original accessory as long as it has a period appearance. A contemporary handlebar fairing, on the other hand, would draw criticism. Restoration by owner Stan Brock.

Left

1938 Four. For beauty of line, it's hard to surpass the right side of the 1938 and later Fours. Note the correct angle of the fork rockers on the bottom of the fork; the upward tilt of about 40 degrees is critical to proper operation. The Four got a completely new motor for 1938, returning to the inlet-over-exhaust (F-Head) layout. Cylinders were cast in pairs instead of individually. Testing revealed that the elimination of some of the air spaces between cylinders allowed heat to more quickly make its way out to the side and into the airstream. Restoration by owner Elmer Lower.

1938 Sport Scout. This restoration includes the popular black-painted cylinders. The full-color Indian-head emblem was first offered on 1938 models. The new large oil pump was also used on the Chief. Restoration by owner Stan Brock.

1938 Four. The 1938 models (except the Junior Scout) had a gray speedometer and ammeter with red lettering plus a gray ignition switch. The black gearshift knob was used on production models.

1938 Four. The traditional leaf-spring fork worked well when new and properly set up. The very strong fork had minimal unsprung weight—only the two small rocker arms and the two connecting rods between the rocker arms and the springs.

continued from page 83

Racing: Harley Fights Back

Harley star Ben Campanale became the first two-time Daytona 200 winner in January. Harleys also won the prestigious Laconia 100-mile TT and the Oakland 200-mile (mile-track) titles. Indian did better in the shorter events where speed was more important than reliability. Two notable Indian victories were Bob Hallowell's Chattanooga, Tennessee, 200-mile TT win on a Chief and Stan Wittinski's victory in the Springfield, Illinois, 25-mile title on the mile-track. These achievements gave Indian the number-one plate for the third consecutive year. Overall, however, Harley had the better year because of its increased attention to the WL series 45 twin. (One of Harley's experiments was to move the side valves closer to the cylinder bores to improve breathing—a copy of an Indian Sport Scout feature. It succeeded in 1939 and became a regular feature for 1940. Harley also increased the inlet-port size on the 1939 racers and again in 1940.)

An important under-the-table development would loom large in Indian's future. Five newly designed Sport Scouts quietly appeared in the hands of favored riders. Although to the casual observer these were typical Sport Scouts, they were actually considerably different. The biggest difference was the larger crankcases, which were designed to reduce crankcase-ventilation problems by reducing the power-robbing air compressor effect in the bottom end. Under the rules of the American Motorcycle Association, these machines should have been declared illegal because Indian didn't comply with the 50-unit-minimum production requirement. The motor numbers of the five big-base Scouts were

1938 Four. The overhead inlet valves were fully enclosed in cast-aluminum compartments, but rocker-arm lubrication was still by air/oil mist. Traditional bore and stroke of 2-3/4 by 3-1/4 inches were retained, keeping displacement at 77.2 ci. All 1938 Fours were delivered with distributor ignition, a departure from the previous practice of offering extra-cost optional magneto spark. The magneto option returned on the 1939 Fours. The black and Chinese Red finish was a no-extra-cost option for 1938, but this example has the extra-cost option of color pattern reversal. Restoration by Vintage Classics; owner: Thomas Baer.

in the 1939 range ("FCI" followed by numbers). These five prewar big-base Sport Scouts were ridden originally by Ed Kretz, Frenchie and Woodsie Castonguay, Ted Edwards, and Lester Hillbish. The machines were returned to Springfield after each big race, and several other riders took turns racing them.

Outside developments impacted Indian development as well. Frank Christian, a gifted motorcycle mechanic, migrated from North Carolina to California, crossing the continent on his Indian Chief, which he proudly claimed would cruise at 100 miles per hour. Word of Christian's claim got around, and contemporaries soon found the boast wasn't idle. The engine was a "stroker," owing its extra urge to the most ancient of hop-up tricks: the lengthening of the stroke. But there were two keys that carried the motorcycle from backyard theory to practical reality. First, there was the availability of the "Z" metal flywheels. Second, British-made Hepolite aluminum-alloy pistons with high silicone content made possible piston speeds that couldn't previously be achieved reliably.

A Decade of Struggle

As the 1930s came to a close, Indian sales were about half of Harley-Davidson's. This actually was an improvement from the early part of the decade when Indian's output was only about a third of Harley's. The credit belongs to Indian President E. Paul du Pont, who restored integrity to the boardroom, and in so doing, turned Indian from a get-rich scheme back into a real motorcycle company.

The author has reviewed the *E. Paul du Pont Papers* maintained by the Research Center of the Henry Ford Museum, and donated to the museum by the du Pont family. Mr. du Pont's letters reveal that he was an enthusiastic motorcyclist, a sharp engineer, and a man who keenly felt his responsibility for the welfare of the employees of the Indian Motocycle Company. These traits, as much as financial planning, were at the center of E. Paul du Pont's efforts to keep Indian alive through the depths of the depression.

Left
1938 Four. The left-hand shift lever and right-hand throttle were frequently requested by customers (right-hand shift and left-hand throttle remained standard Indian practice). The 1938 Chief, Four, and Sport Scout featured a fork shield, those of the Chief and Four being identical, as they shared a common fork. The shield is just above the leaf springs.

1938 Junior Scout. Among the major differences between the 30.50-ci twin and the Prince were the crankcase, cylinder heads, cylinders, distributor ignition, and dry-sump (recirculating) oil pump.

Left

1938 Junior Scout. The little twin formerly known as the Scout Pony became the Junior Scout in 1937. The Prince roots of the Scout Pony, Junior Scout, and Thirty-Fifty, as it became known in 1940, are evident. Many of the components were direct carryovers from the defunct Prince. These included forks, frame, generator drive and cover, primary drive and cover, clutch, and transmission. Along with other 1938 models, the Junior Scout had the horn mounted above the headlight. The bayonet filler tank caps had arrived on the little twin in 1937 and on other Indians in 1936. Restoration by Elmer Lower.

1939 Four. This 1939 Four is unrestored except for a new carburetor, inlet manifold, and exhaust manifold. The plumbing from the exhaust manifold to the carburetor has been removed because the heat-riser setup rusted rapidly. The World's Fair paint scheme was a new option on the 1939 models, along with the "V" panel. The Metallic Blue and silver combination was new. Except for silver, 1939 was the first year that metallic paints were offered. Owner: Leon Blackman.

Right
1939 Sport Scout. *Combustion-chamber efficiency was assured with a true Y-shaped inlet manifold and companion cylinders, features which dated from mid-1935. According to former factory engineer Jimmy Hill, combustion-chamber flow-testing was accomplished on the 1934 prototype with the assistance of the Massachusetts Institute of Technology.*

1939 Sport Scout. *Striking looks from any angle, this 1939 Sport Scout is finished in Metallic Sand Taupe and Chinese Red. The paint scheme features Chinese Red World's Fair tank panels. The chrome-plated upswept tail pipe was new for 1939. Reproduction period saddlebags and luggage rack are nice touches. A 1939 advertisement shouted, "Indian holds eight out of the twelve new official stock motorcycle records . . . When you ride an Indian, you ride a winner." Restoration by owner Pete Sink.*

Top
1939 Sport Scout. *Finally, an air cleaner was provided in 1939 instead of the gravel-straining air horn. Note the clip securing the oil-tank breather tube to the frame front down tube. Small parts such as these were cadmium plated in 1939; previously, they had been nickel plated.*

An Era Ends and a War Begins

1940–1945

The du Pont-Hosley team that had managed Indian since 1930 came to an end in February 1940 when Joe Hosley died of a heart attack. After Hosley's death, du Pont never seemed to regain the enthusiasm he had once felt for Indian. With most of the world already at war, Indian enjoyed booming business due to both military sales and a restless civilian populace that sensed that the days of peace in the United States might soon end. Indian's 1940 production totaled 10,431 machines, which included 5,000 Chiefs built for the French army. This was as close as the post-1926 Indian company ever came to matching Harley-Davidson, which sold 10,855 units, almost all civilian models. In addition to motorcycle production, Indian operated a training school in the Wigwam for Army motorcycle mechanics. Indian's profits soared to $703,000.

1940: Skirts and Springs

Indian startled American enthusiasts by introducing skirted fenders, full chain guards, and rear suspension for the 1940 lineup. All models got the skirts, while the spring frame was limited to the Chief and the Four. The Chief and Sport Scout also received new streamlined cylinders and cylinder heads. The little twin previously called the Junior Scout was renamed the "Thirty-Fifty," a nickname derived from its 30.50-ci displacement.

The fender skirts were a love-it-or-hate-it proposition.

Working alongside Ed Kretz in the Los Angeles Indian shop of Floyd Clymer, was Frank Christian. With the impending dealership takeover by Johnson Motors in late 1939, Christian recalled, "I just could not wait to get out of Clymer's, to get to that other place with all those new Indians with them skirted fenders—beautiful things!" Desert enduro rider and speed-run artist Max Bubeck, a close friend of Kretz and Christian, had a different view of the skirted fender Indians. "That's when Indian stopped making motorcycles and started making Harleys," Bubeck objected. His

continued on page 97

Top
1941 Sport Scout. *Two-color finishes were cataloged for the 1941 models. The five standard combinations were: red and white, blue and white, black and white, red and black, and blue and black. This restoration is in Fallon Brown and red, an interpretation of Indian's long running policy of extra-cost special finishes. The 1941 models had a new horn face.*

Far left
1941 Sport Scout. *Handsome, streamlined cylinders were introduced on the 1940 Sport Scout and Chief. From a 1941 advertisement, ". . . beautiful 45 cubic inch engine and quick acceleration that challenges your every whim." Restoration by owner Elmer Lowler.*

Left
1941 Sport Scout. *These streamlined saddlebags were brought out for the 1940 season.*

1940 Chief. *Streamlined cylinders and heads graced the 1940 Chief and Sport Scout. Inside, the cylinder heads had the same shape as the 1939 heads. Many of what Indian called "clips," the small brackets used with wiring, gas lines, and oil lines, were finished in black in 1940. A black clip is at the top front of the rear spring.*

Right
1940 Chief. *For 1940 only, the Chief, Four, and Sport Scout used a black toolbox. The toolbox was mounted differently on each model. On the Chief, the toolbox was forward of the primary-drive case. Restoration by owner Tom Gadd.*

1941 Sport Scout. *Weighing in at 500 pounds, the 1941 Sport Scout was 115 pounds beefier than the original 1934 version. To restore some of the former get up and go, some riders installed Harley-Davidson Forty-five flywheels which had a longer stroke. This produced a 49.5-ci (811-cc) engine. For even more low-end grunt, cut-down Chief flywheels yielded 57.6 ci (944 cc).*

The Wigwam

The giant Indian factory known as the Wigwam was located about 1 mile east of downtown Springfield, Massachusetts, near the intersection of State Street (left side of the factory) and Wilbraham road (right side of the factory). The address was 837 State Street. The small, three-story building at the lower part of the "V" shape is a fire station, which was built on ground called Winchester Park a few years after Indian moved to this location. Behind the fire station is a four-story section that has six windows facing Wilbraham road. The left half of this section—the State Street half with the large sign on the roof—and the long part of the building on State Street down to the first elevator tower was the extent of the premises that Indian first occupied in 1906. These original Indian State Street premises had previously been the first vocational high school in the United States.

Although this photo was taken about 1935, it's representative of the factory during the years 1919 through 1948.

Earlier, the Indian factory consisted of a smaller building on Worthington Street in the center of the city. The move to State Street was in conjunction with the termination of a contract with the Aurora Manufacturing Company of Aurora, Illinois, for the manufacture of Hedstrom-designed Indian motorcycle engines. Once in the Wigwam, Indian built its own motors.

The original State Street factory had 74,000 square feet, and was of red brick with wooden beams and flooring. This construction scheme was retained for all subsequent enlargements. In 1910, the factory was enlarged more than 50 percent by doubling the size of the section behind the fire station (which brought its south side over to Wilbraham Road) and by adding a wing along Wilbraham Road. This added 46,000 square feet and gave the distinctive "V" or wigwam shape to the complex. The third and final stage of construction went on more or less continuously between 1910 and 1913, and continued in spurts through 1919. Prior to his resignation in 1913, cofounder Oscar Hedstrom was the principal designer for these

expansions. During some of these expansions, both motorcycle manufacturing and building construction continued around the clock, with drop cloths used to separate motorcycle builders from the out of doors. The Wigwam was intended to produce 60,000 motorcycles per year.

Ironically, the factory reached its full size just as the first sales slump hit the American motorcycle industry. By 1933, the Wigwam was operating at only 5 percent of capacity! In only four of the 17 post-1930 production years did Indian production rise above 10,000 units. When Ralph Rogers took over Indian, he deemed the factory obsolete and moved production to east Springfield buildings that had been used by Indian during WWI.

In the 1940 business year, Indian produced 10,855 units, and in the 1941 business year they produced 18,428 units. The business years ran from October through September. Specific year models were made from about July through June, so each business and calendar year included two different model years, and each model year

spanned two different calendar and business years. Consequently, we don't know how many 1940 and 1941 models were made. In fact, we don't even know how many motorcycles were made! What was a "unit"? Did they count sidecars?

Referring again to the aerial view of the Wigwam, the following was the general production scheme. The administrative and management offices were in the northwest end of the factory along State Street and behind the fire station. The top floor of the area behind the fire station contained the experimental department. Raw materials such as bar stock and bulk supplies such as tires, were stored in the basement rooms along State Street. The heaviest operations, such as punch presses and machining of large items, were done on the ground floor. Production then moved generally toward Wilbraham Road then upward and around the complex in a counter-clockwise direction. Final assembly was in the top floor of the State Street wing just east of the railroad tracks that split the complex.

The total area of the Wigwam was more than 400,000 square feet or nine acres. If each floor were laid end to end the factory would be about 1-1/2 miles long and 100 feet wide. Near its maximum size and staff in 1915, the Wigwam could build 300 motorcycles per day. The maximum output peaked in the 1913 business year, with 32,000 units produced. According to *Largest Motorcycle Business In The World,* a 1915 factory publication, an order for 35,000 motorcycles required the following supplies: 1,200,000 feet of tubing, 47 carloads of tires, 10,000 gallons of paint, 285,000 feet of chain, 270 tons of spring steel, 15 tons of brazing spelter, 1,364,000 feet of lumber for packing, 250 tons of aluminum castings, and 208 tons of bronze castings.

continued from page 93

specific complaint was the extra weight added by the new fenders, wheels, and rear suspension. For example, the skirted-fender Chief was listed at 558 pounds dry, while the 1939 Chief was listed at 482 pounds.

Racing

Score 1940 racing as a draw between Indian and Harley-Davidson. Melvin Rhoades won the Springfield, Illinois, 25-Mile National Championship, the Wigwam's fourth consecutive 25-mile title and consequent number-one plate assignment. Ed Kretz accomplished his third Langhorne 100 victory, and Ted Edwards won two national championship TT events on a 74-ci Chief. Much was made of Edwards's praise of the plunger rear suspension on his Chief. Important Harley-Davidson progress was made with the new WLDR. Harley rider Babe Tancrede won the Daytona 200 and the Laconia 100, and Louis Guanella won the 200-mile Oakland, California, title.

In amateur competition, Frank Chase and Max Bubeck came on the scene in southern California speed trials. Their stoker Chief, inspired by Frank Christian's cross-country machine, turned 128.5 miles per hour.

1941

Changes were few for 1941. The only major changes were the Sport Scout's spring frame and the Thirty-Fifty's use of open fenders instead of skirted. Other changes to the 1941 model line were in the details. Indian built 8,739 motorcycles at a profit of $381,000 while Harley-Davidson built 18,428 machines.

The machines from Milwaukee dominated racing, too. After the Sport Scout's control of Class C flat track racing for most of the late 1930s, Harley-Davidson countered with first the WLDR in 1940, then in 1941 with the brakeless WR for flat tracking and the braked WRTT for road racing and TT races. The WR and WRTT were Milwaukee's first out-of-the-box production racers; riders no longer had to bother unbolting lights and road-model fenders, or removing brakes for flat tracking.

At Daytona, the 200-mile championship fell to Norton rider Billy Mathews—a preview of the "British invasion" that would revolutionize American motorcycling in the postwar period. All five of Indian's "big base" Sport Scouts retired.

End of an Era

The 1940 season had brought the dramatic changes of skirted fenders and rear suspension. The Indian factory had enjoyed its highest production rates in years. At the end of 1941 with the uncertainty of a world war at hand, Indian and its tribes of dealers and riders didn't understand the pivotal nature of the season just past. The 1941 season would be the last full season

Getting to the Races

Although the United States didn't enter World War II until December 1941, throughout the year, American heavy industry was engaged in military production on behalf of Britain and its allies. Desert enduro rider and speed-trials expert Max Bubeck had signed on with Lockheed aircraft. Jimmy Kelly, an up-and-coming Sport Scout racer, worked for Brauncorp, a defense subcontractor. Both Bubeck and Kelly put in a lot of overtime, which was typical in the defense industry. The heavy work schedules made getting to the race meets a challenge. Here are Bubeck's and Ed Kretz's recollections of traveling from the Los Angeles area to northern California for a race meet:

Bubeck: "It was about a five-hour drive from Los Angeles to Fresno, but we never could leave before 12:30 AM because we had to pick Jimmy Kelly up. He worked swing shifts at Brauncorp in Alhambra. He'd get off at 12:30, and Ed would have the machines loaded already. I'd get over to Ed's house, and we'd leave from there, pick up Kelly, and we were on our way. Kelly was a Long Beach motorcycle cop in later years. We'd usually get into Tiny's Waffle Shop in Fresno about 6:00 in the morning."

Kretz: "Do you remember the time we sent Kelly into town for that Chrysler, when something blew up?"

Bubeck: "We didn't send him; we just kept playing cards while he was griping and carrying on. There were five of us in the car, playing cards . . . we used to play cards all the time. Kelly was driving, and it was just getting light. We were about 20 miles from Fresno, and the drive shaft went out. It had been rattling and carrying on something awful, and it finally just quit. So we're parked there, and Kelly said, 'Well, what are we going to do?' We just kept on playing cards and ignored him. So, Kelly got out, and the next thing we knew, we hear his motorcycle starting up—and it's all set up for half-mile racing, no brakes, no lights, nothing. Twenty miles into Fresno, he rode. About an hour later he came back with Hap Alzina. Hap got out a rope and hitched to us, and we had a big caravan going. We used to be pretty indifferent. The guy who was driving was in charge of the ship, and everyone else did what he wanted."

1940 Indian Sales Catalog.
"Style-blazers of the motorcycle world—the new 1940 Indians with their matchless sweeping beauty, graceful full skirted fenders, dashing chrome trim, and unbeatable dependability."

of multiple-model production. The classic Four and the race-winning Sport Scout would see only token production in the few weeks of the 1942 season. With hindsight, the 1940 and 1941 seasons are seen today as truly the end of an era.

The War Years

For more than two years after the beginning of WWII, from September 1939 and into December 1941, the United States had been a neutral power. But throughout this period, the federal government and American industry did all they could to assist Britain and her allies against the Germans. For example, there was an official willingness to sell armament to any of the warring nations, but with the proviso that the belligerents had to pick up the merchandise in the United States and arrange for their own shipments. The practical effect was to exclude Germany, which could hardly cross an Atlantic heavily policed by the British Navy. In a mockery of the official policy, *Life*, the nation's most popular magazine, ran a full page photo of a group of smiling Canadians pulling a freshly built American fighter plane across the border between Washington state and Canada.

The point is: since 1939, a massive defense-industry buildup had been in progress aimed at helping the Allied Powers, and everybody knew it. The federal government stepped into the economy and rationed steel, aluminum, magnesium, rubber, and dozens of other commodities needed for defense production. Indian and Harley-Davidson quickly learned that they couldn't count on the necessary raw materials to satisfy military motorcycle orders, let alone make pleasure motorcycles.

When the shooting war started for the United States in December 1941, *continued on page 103*

continued on page 103

1940 police Chief. A friendlier view of a police Indian. This example is equipped with the winter windshield apron.

Right
1940 police Chief. A troubling view when these lights were lit! The Pennsylvania patrol had 602 Indians on duty in 1940, and New York City used 480 Chiefs. A complete listing of Indian-mounted state and local departments would fill several pages in this book. Restoration by Starklite Cycle; owner: Bob Stark.

Indian Trains Army Mechanics

This photo appeared in the April 1941 *Motorcyclist*, but it could have been made as early as 1939 when Indian opened its factory Army mechanic's school. Erle "Pop" Armstrong was the only instructor. Said *Motorcyclist*, "With the normal dealers' mechanics service schools over for 1941, the Indian school has been turned into a training center for Army men. Students are, in the latest classes, taught the fundamentals of motorcycle mechanics and the rudiments of teaching others. At present a new four week course has been inaugurated that includes instructions in the art of riding as well as maintenance. At the completion of all courses, the Army man is now taught how to teach others to ride motorcycles. While these courses, naturally, do not make expert riders they do furnish a foundation upon which to build with experience."

In 1941, two more instructors were hired, Jack Neiss and James "Jimmy" Hill. In 1942, the Army mechanic's school was moved to Springfield College. The 1942 instructional staff was increased by two civilian instructors and three Army instructors. By this time, nearly a thousand Army men had attended the Indian school. Incoming students without previous motorcycle experience were given the basic course; experienced students were given more advanced training. All Indian military models—the 340, 640B, 741, and 841—were studied.

1941, Indian mechanics at the factory school. *Jimmy Hill.*

1940 police Chief. *The long arm of the law favored Indians over Harleys. In 1940, 70 percent of the nation's population was patrolled by Indian motorcycles. This California Highway Patrol Indian had tribal brothers in the state patrols of Maryland, Massachusetts, North Carolina, Pennsylvania, Texas, and of course many others.*

1940 Four. *The impressive-looking rear suspension was not as effective as it would appear. Half the springs were below the axle to damp rebound. Still, the rider got a much better ride than with a rigid frame.*

1940 Four. *In the opinion of some, the skirted fender Fours were the best-looking Indians ever made. This one is painted Jade green, a color that was listed in the press release for Motorcyclist magazine but not listed in the earlier-printed 1940 sales catalogs. Other 1940 colors described by Motorcyclist but not in the 1940 sales catalog were Kashan Green (blue-green) and Fallon Brown (beige). Restoration by Bollenbach Engineering.*

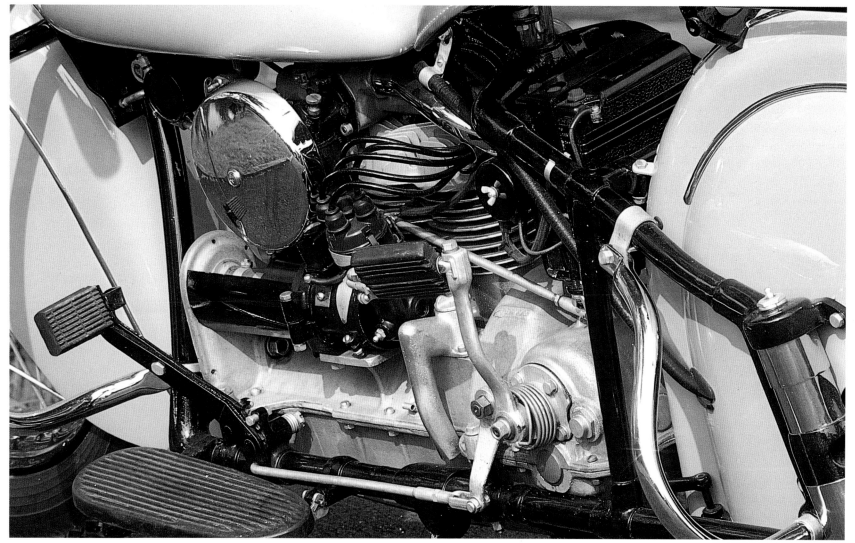

1940 Four. *The less attractive (some might say cluttered) left side of the Four is a cultivated taste. Imaginary X-ray vision helps, as there really is a good-looking engine hiding behind the carburetor and electrical stuff of this battery-ignition model. Magneto-ignition Four engines were even more obscured.*

continued from page 99

Indian and Harley-Davidson weren't surprised. Both companies had been selling ever-increasing orders of motorcycles to the U.S. Army, as well as to the Allied Powers. Indian and Harley-Davidson had been involved in large-scale Army training maneuvers, and both companies had designed and delivered prototype shaft-drive motorcycles for Army testing.

In 1940, the Germans had brilliantly executed their blitzkrieg war of mobility, subduing supposedly impregnable France in about a month. Motorcycles figured prominently in German operations, so with the United States in the war at last, Indian and Harley-Davidson expected huge motorcycle orders for the U.S. Army. Unfortunately, neither company could foresee the four-wheeled Jeeps that would relegate the American motorcycle to behind-the-lines administrative duties.

1942: Few New Motorcycles

On the West Coast, distributor Hap Alzina announced in a November 5, 1941, bulletin that 1942 Fours would only be provided to West Coast dealers to fill police orders and that the Thirty-Fifty would not be available as a 1942 model on the West Coast. Alzina went on:

No authoritative information is available on possible arrival date of 1942 models into the warehouses. With the raw material situation as it is, neither distributor or factory is in a position to hazard a guess as to when machines for normal dealer and civilian consumption can be built.

PRIORITY RATINGS OR PREFERENCE CERTIFICATES are a "MUST" on all police orders if any reasonable delivery is to be

1940 Sport Scout. *The two-color finish wasn't cataloged as a 1940 option. Both the Sport Scout and the little twin, now renamed the Thirty-Fifty, had skirted fenders but rigid frames. Restoration by Paul Pearce.*

expected, and dealers should be explicit in bringing this point to the attention of any police department they may have been dealing with. Delivery is almost impossible without some sort of priority and will be as prompt as the priority rating is potent. . .

Obviously, very few 1942-model civilian Indians were built. No 1942-model sales literature was produced, which indicates that pessimism had already set in by late summer 1941. In the first place, production of 1942 models during late 1941 was hampered by material shortages caused by defense industry priorities. Though the United States didn't enter the war until December 7, by the time of the Alzina bulletin the federal government had already taken over all strategic economic decisions. Meeting minutes from the Harley-Davidson board of directors indicate that in mid-1941 Harley-Davidson experienced a four-month delay in receiving the steel required to complete a priority defense contract for motorcycles for the

Canadian Army. Civilian-motorcycle manufacturing was therefore even more difficult. On February 9, 1942, the federal government halted all civilian vehicle production.

The exact specifications of the few 1942 civilian Indians are unknown. Sketchy information in the form of photos in *Indian News* and a single dealer bulletin provide some data. An indian-head emblem was placed on the tanks; this is the same emblem seen on 1946 Chiefs. Miscellaneous parts formerly chrome plated were changed to enamel finish. Some 1941 motor numbers were used on 1942 models after October 3, 1941 (normally all models in production would be assigned motor numbers for the next model year).

On May 3, the national speed limit was set at 40 miles per hour, mainly to lessen tire wear. On May 17, gasoline supplies in 17 eastern states were cut by 50 percent. The national speed limit was later lowered to 35 miles per hour. On December 1, nationwide gasoline rationing began.

1941 Four. *The four-cylinder Indian that started out as the 455-pound Ace had now grown up to be the 568-pound, spring-frame Indian Four. Bigger tires further added to the feeling of weight. Power output had climbed from about 30 horsepower to about 40 horsepower, perhaps keeping performance at an even keel, perhaps not. Most Americans thought bigger was better, so the skirted-fender Fours fit right in.*

1941 Chief. *For 1941, Indian reluctantly gave in to popular demand and made these 5.00x16-inch tires available as a no-cost option. The 5.00x16-inch tires didn't work as well with the rear springs. Unrestored motorcycles such as this one are growing in favor and prestige, and some enthusiasts (such as the author) believe it is a sacrilege to restore such complete and original examples. Unrestored bikes are a treasure trove of information for those who are restoring same or similar machines. Owner: Doug Van Allen.*

War Games for
Kretz, Chase, and Bubeck

Kretz and the Army

Ed Kretz recalls his wartime jobs: "I went to the factory and tested the shaft-drive jobs [the 841 Model] when I worked for the government. I was an instructor at the Army camp in Pomona [California], where I taught riding and motorcycle mechanics, mostly on Indians but on Harleys, too. I did that for two years, and they wanted me to go to Atlanta and run this school. But I said I didn't want to leave California."

"Then, they gave me a job traveling in this sidecar shaft-drive outfit, and I went all over, even up into Canada to check the Harley and Indian dealers over there, all on government time. I did that for about a year. I went out to the desert, out beyond Yuma in that Army camp. They had a little school there, and I went out to see if they needed any help. Then I went to Ogden, Utah, and Salt Lake. The Indian shaft drives, and the Harleys too, never got out of the States. They built them for Tunisia, for the sand dunes, but they never did leave."

Chase and Bubeck

Frank Chase and Max Bubeck weren't called to war, as both were a little over the ripest age for the draft; additionally, Bubeck was working in the defense industry. In their spare time, the duo decided to shoehorn their Chief engine into a Series 101 Scout frame, thus creating a "Chout." Bubeck modified the motor with some porting modifications, polished the valves, and shaped the cylinder heads. Chase took care of the meticulous chore of achieving as near perfect balance as possible. Both men worked on the magneto to obtain precisely correct ignition timing on both cylinders. Strangely, stock Indian magnetos varied by as much as 1/8 inch of cylinder stroke (front cylinder versus rear cylinder) as to when they produced a spark. This was one reason why a few stock Indians were exceptionally fast and why a few were exceptionally slow—such oddballs were on opposite extremes of the randomly manufactured Indians. On the Chout, the unacceptable ignition condition was eliminated by careful grinding of the magneto cam. The engine was stroked to 4-13/16 inches, yielding 78 ci (1280 cc).

After running the Chout for a while as a stroker, the boys decided to get patriotic. There was a wartime movement afoot to de-emphasize speed as a hobby, and in a gesture of compliance, the Chout was brought back to its original 74 ci. Even in this lower displacement guise, the Chout turned over 109 miles per hour, beating the next fastest bike in under-the-table speed trials by more than 7 miles per hour.

Military production dominated in 1942, with only a dribble of civilian 1942 models produced in late 1941 and early 1942. Indian produced 16,647 machines in 1942 and earned $1.1 million, the largest profit of the E. Paul du Pont era. Naturally, the war years were tough on dealers.

Only one of the thousands of Model 741, 30.50-ci, side-valve V-twin models was sold directly to the U.S. Army. However, many 741s passed through U.S. Army hands as part of lend-lease arrangements with Allied powers. The Model 741 was sold in large numbers to Canada and other British Commonwealth nations, which favored its 500-cc side-valve engine.

1943

In 1943, Indian was granted the Army-Navy Production Award, commonly referred to as the "E" award for excellence, symbolized by the "E" banner presented. Local radio personality and Indian rider Bob Steele acted as master of ceremonies. Representing the Army was Brigadier General Lewis. Accepting the "E" banner were Indian Vice President and General Manager Dwight L. Moody, and 31-year-employee John Bible. President E. Paul du Pont delivered a brief message. Cofounder George Hendee had recently died, but fellow cofounder Oscar Hedstrom was present. Also in attendance was the legendary Cannonball Baker. For the business year 1943, Indian earned a profit of $398,000. With 1943 production of 16,456 machines, the net profit per motorcycle was just $24, or roughly 5 percent.

On a less cheery note, G. Briggs Weaver, the engineer and stylist who had penned the famous skirted fenders, had left the Wigwam. He was busy designing a series of "modular" motorcycles for the Torque Manufacturing Company of Plainfield, Connecticut. These motorcycles would be of different displacements but would share as many components as possible. Weaver envisioned a lighter range of motorcycles than what Indian and Harley-Davidson had been building, a range technically abreast of advanced lightweight and medium-weight British and European models. Weaver's concept called for overhead-valves and engines of one, two, and four cylinders. Weaver's drawing board was destined to again influence the Wigwam in the postwar years.

1944

In June, the War Production Board authorized production of 1,700 Model 345 motorcycles for essential police and civilian use. For the year, production totaled 3,881 machines. Harley-Davidson built 17,006 motorcycles of which some 15,000 were targeted for military use.

Gasoline rationing was cut to two gallons per week, but crafty riders and dealers found ways around the rationing. Some rigged their motorcycles to run on cleaning solvent, albeit rather poorly. "We cleaned a lot of parts!" chuckled Ed Kretz. Surprisingly, synthetic motorcycle tires lasted up

continued on page 110

Circa 1941 Sport Scout racer.
Sport Scout racers like this were used by Indian riders to dominate half-mile stock motorcycle racing in the mid-1930s. By 1941, the Harley-Davidson WR had caught up at the top level of expert racing. But large numbers of Sport Scout racing motorcycles were in the hands of novice- and amateur-class riders, and average Sport Scouts seemed to have an edge on average pre-1941 Harleys. Restoration by Starklite Cycle.

Circa 1941 Sport Scout racer.
The Indian-Harley racing battles caught the attention of Harley-Davidson board member William H. Davidson, who in 1936 reported to the board, that the Sport Scout ". . . seemed to be a better job than ours." Harley-Davidson, however, had better quality control than Indian. Record-setting Indian tuner Red Fenwick (rider, Fred Ludlow) used Harley connecting rods, and Indian's top star Ed Kretz used a Harley crankpin. Said Kretz, "Indian rollers—you could buy a thousand rollers and get about 300 different sizes. I miked every roller that I put in."

Model 640B. *The Model 640B Army motorcycle was basically a Sport Scout gone to war. Few were built. Owner: Robin Markey.*

Model 640B. *The Model 640B featured a cast-aluminum duct from the air cleaner to the carburetor.*

Model 841. *The Model 841 Army motorcycle perhaps had its inception at the 1939 World's Fair in New York City. There, E. Paul du Pont purchased a BMW and became enthused about shaft drive. E. Paul prepared some of the Model 841 engineering drawings himself, though entrusting most of the work to engineer Allan Carter.*

Model 841. *The Model 841 tank panel included a green generator-charge warning light and a red oil-pressure warning light.*

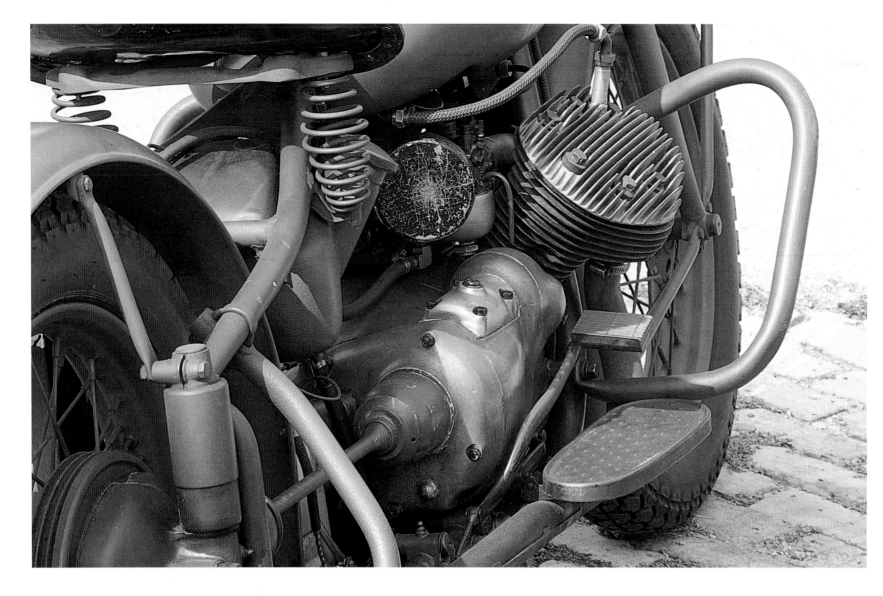

continued from page 106

to 30,000 miles. Unfortunately, these tires were about as hard as wood, recalled Max Bubeck, and offered almost no traction when wet.

Indian's wartime advertisements packed nostalgia and hope. In December 1944, an artist's rendition of two Indian riders high on a hilltop appeared. Their headlights split the night air, while a small town's signature steepled community church rested quietly below. Beneath the picture were these words: "Silvered Steeple Ahead. A world of pleasure is in store for the rider of Tomorrow's Indian. There will be health and adventure, too, when victory is won. Plan to get out in the open on your future and perfect Indian. . . . Its brilliant, unexcelled, battle-ground performances have won the praises and preferences of thousands on every fighting front. Let us tell you about some of the wonderful days that are not far off, when Indian's new postwar champion will make motorcycling an even greater and more economical travel pleasure . . . Buy War Bonds now to buy an Indian later."

1945

In August, with the war over, the Wigwam work week was cut from 60 to 48 hours. The past 15 du Pont years (excludes 1930—no available data) totaled a cumulative production of 91,052 Indians compared to Harley's cumulative production of over 196,000 machines during the same period. Cumulative du Pont era losses totaled $260,000. Tired of the financial roller coaster ride, du Pont sought a buyer for the Indian Motocycle Company.

After a false start with an outfit called Lawrance Aeronautical in November 1945, E. Paul du Pont and his brother Francis sold their controlling interests to a group headed by Ralph B. Rogers. Rogers' aim was to build a line of lightweight European-style motorcycles, which he was convinced would sell in large numbers. Annual production for 1945 totaled 2,070 Chiefs. Harley-Davidson built over 10,000 bikes.

110

Left

Model 841. *The Model 841 was powered by a 45 ci side-valve V-twin that owed its cylinder and cylinder-head design to the Sport Scout. Though it's hard to visualize, 90-degree V-twins are inherently smooth, even as smooth as horizontally opposed twins. Ninety-degree V-twins are smooth because each cylinder makes oscillating and reciprocating forces that are 90 degrees out of phase with each other. These forces are exactly counterbalanced by the companion cylinder because of the 90-degree angle between the cylinders.*

Model 841. *The speedometer has about double the required capability. Harley and Indian each built 1,000 motorcycles, Model XA and Model 841 respectively, for comparative testing purposes. Following a year and a half of testing, on July 3, 1943, the Army canceled all plans for large-scale production of either the Indian or Harley shaft-drive machines.*

1943 Model 741

During 1939 and 1940, Indian competed with Harley-Davidson and the Delco corporation in Army motorcycle test programs. Indian's left-hand throttle was preferred over the others' right hand throttle, the theory being that this would enable couriers to more easily hand off message packets. Harley-Davidson handlebars were preferred, and Harley fenders worked best because their large tire clearance kept wheels from becoming locked up in accumulated mud. In water crossings, Harleys also showed up best. Motor relia-

1943 Model 741

bility was considered a draw among the competitors. By a wide margin, the Harley-Davidson factory was considered best for large-scale motorcycle production. As a result of these factors, Harley-Davidson was awarded almost all military motorcycle contracts for U.S. forces during WWII.

To bolster worker and dealer morale, Indian featured many photos of Army Indians under test and in maneuvers. The frequently shown military Indian photos were of Indians left over from contracted test programs, or photos of Model 741 motorcycles that were part of a Lend-Lease (barter) pool awaiting distribution to Allied forces. Indian's total motorcycle production for 1942 through 1945 was 39,000; Harley-Davidson's was 85,000.

One factor working against Indian in the military competition may have been its Model 741 engine, which at 30.50 ci was two-thirds the size of the Harley 45 engine. However, Allied nations included the 30.50-ci capacity in their specifications, so Indian was able to win several motorcycle contracts for British Empire nations and others. As a result, there are still many Model 741 motorcycles tooling around Australia and New Zealand.

A Race In Mexico

The American Motorcycle Association didn't sanction any races during the war. This didn't stop hard-core racers, of course, who circumvented the problem by heading south of the border. Ed Kretz and Max Bubeck recalled the Mexican race:

Kretz: "During the war, there were some races down in Mexico. I won the only one I went to, which was in Enseñda, on the beach."

Bubeck: "Yeah . . . after you got through throwing up just before it started."

Kretz: "Yeah, I was really sick. Boy, I was miserable."

Bubeck: "Well, you spent most of the night in the jail, didn't you?"

Kretz: "No, they got Louie Thomas. They beat the hell out of Louie, thinking he was me. It was my fault. We were all dancing, and a couple of women went into the ladies' room, and I followed 'em in. That was the wrong thing to do. These Mexican guys grabbed me, and I was just knocking the hell out of 'em. Brad Cohen, who was up in Frisco—his daughter Phyllis was there. She said, 'Get out of here! Get out of here!' Oscar and Johnny Sherman said the same thing and added that the cops were going to get me.

"Well, they got me out of the joint, and I was going down the street. I wanted to go back, but they were smarter and kept me out-side. Pretty soon, the Mexicans got Louie Thomas. We both had Royal Rider T-shirts on, and Louie was about my size. They grabbed him, put him in this old Model A Ford, and figuring that he would try to get out, banged him on the head—just beat the hell out of him, and about wrecked his eyes. They took him into jail, thinking that he was me, but I was safe, thanks to Oscar and Phyllis getting me out of there. I got home in the motel, and boy, I was sick!

"Anyway, I won that race and Floyd Emde got second. I remember Burton Albrecht was with us, and he would help me a lot. The Mexicans had little poles to mark the course, and I was going around a little too far out, so in the heat race some guys were coming under me a little bit. So Burton told me to stay in there, closer to the inside, but I knocked the hell out of my fingers. I was hitting those damned poles with my fingers. I was laid over quite a bit, and my wheels were maybe four feet out. But at the time, it didn't bother me because I was still leading. Those Mexicans all bet on who was going to win. After the race—goddam! They came over and you would've thought I was an old-time buddy of theirs. They put their arms around me and bragged about the $3 or so that they'd won on me. I got about $40 for winning."

Customized Model 841.
Civilianized Model 841 Indians have been built by a number of enthusiasts. Restoration by owner Wally Krzyzanowski.

Model 344 Chief. *For police departments, Indian made a few wartime Chiefs like this Navy Blue example. White or gray tanks, fenders, and chain guards were also available, but silver paint wasn't an option because it contained scarce aluminum. Nonskirted fenders were considered less wasteful than the full-skirted fenders. The Indian Model 340 (military Chief) used the nonskirted fenders as well. During 1945, the government eased restrictions and permitted a few Chiefs to be built for verified essential civilian transportation, like back and forth between home and a bomber plant. An extraordinary amount of paper work was required for both police and essential civilian orders. Owner: Randy Chandrasena.*

Ecstasy and Agony

1946–1949

From December 1941 through August 1945, American motorcycling had been in hibernation. With the grim business of WWII finally behind, tens of thousands of former motorcyclists eagerly looked ahead to the shedding of their military uniforms and a return to the motorcycling fun they had known before the war. Additionally, another multitude of youngsters had reached the age when they might be recruited by motorcycle shops instead of Uncle Sam.

The war's end had a huge impact on the imaginations and the emotions of American youth. Of America's leisure pursuits, only baseball had continued in the national limelight at every level from school yards to the big stadiums of storied teams. Like their baseball counterparts, Indian and Harley-Davidson fans were each fiercely loyal to their "teams." Together Harley and Indian had won 90 percent of all American motorcycle races ever run. In December 1941, the motorcycle teams had folded after a string of some 40 years of success. Here the analogy is faulty, however, because athletics continued during the war, whereas motorcycling was, in effect, prohibited by the war. Baseball fans could've known motorcyclists' sense of loss only if baseball had been outlawed at every level during the war.

The war had put dreams on hold. With peace finally returned, there were tremendous stored up pressures to enjoy peacetime pursuits to the fullest. The Indian and Harley-Davidson factories and dealers salivated over their renewed opportunities. Dozens of former motorcycle racers itched to get back out on the tracks. These prewar racers knew they had a unique margin of experience over young racers just entering the sport. But the

Top
Ex-Floyd Emde 1948 Model 648 Scout. *For the 1948 racing season, the Wigwam built either 50 complete Model 648 Scouts, or they built 25 complete motorcycles and another 25 engines. Choose your favorite story. Anyway, San Diego rider Floyd Emde rode this particular 648 to victory in the 1948 Daytona 200, the nation's most prestigious race.*

Far left
1948 Model 648 Scout. *On the Model 648, the Edison Splitdorf magneto was moved from the rear of the primary drive to the oil pump. This provided more accurate timing by the elimination of the backlash that had been previously present through the primary drive chain. The best racing Sport Scouts would turn over 7000 revolutions per minute, and run up to about 115 miles per hour with road-race gearing. Restoration by owner Jim Sutter.*

Left
Model 648 Scout. *The English Terry saddle was standard. As usual with V-twin Indians, the gearshift lever could be fitted for left-hand operation, shown here, or fitted for traditional right-hand operation. The separate oil tank left more room for fuel in the twin top-side tanks. The Model 648 Scout was commonly referred to as the "big-base" Scout or as the Daytona Scout. The term "big-base" arose from the larger crankcase volume achieved by squaring out the rear of the crankcase with an enlarged oil sump. The larger crankcase volume reduced the air compressor effect.*

1946 Chief. The main change for 1946 was the new girder fork. As usual, Indian didn't document the whole story. The first batch of 1946 Chiefs were finished in black only, according to Indian News. This example has Navy Blue tanks, fenders, and chain guard, based on observation of unrestored machines. The 1946 catalog listed red, black, and police silver as the only colors.

largest group of players in the resumed game of motorcycling were the hundreds of thousands of potential first-time motorcyclists. Instead of one year's supply of high school graduates, the pool of motorcycle prospects was five times that size. They also had more money in their pockets than any group of prewar motorcycling prospects. Motorcycling was about to enjoy an explosion of growth and enthusiasm.

1946: The Chief Soldiers on Alone

Because Indian was financially weak, only the Chief remained in the 1946 Indian lineup. Even so, with so much pent-up demand for new motorcycles, Indian couldn't build too many Chiefs. The major Chief update was a new hydraulically damped girder fork derived from the military shaft-drive Model 841. Chief production for 1946 totaled 6,974 units compared to Harley-Davidson's total of 15,554. This comparison differs from those previously presented, which compared Indian and Harley-Davidson fiscal years, and is presented differently here because almost half the 1946-model sales occurred from September through December 1946, which were part of Indian's fiscal year 1947. Production was continually hampered by supplier problems with castings and heat treating; many items failed to meet Indian's acceptance inspections. These problems delayed the ramp up in production required to compensate for Indian's minimal 1945 motorcycle production. Engineering efforts continued on a planned postwar Sport Scout, which was to be equipped with the Chief's front fork, rear generator drive, and modified Chief rear suspension.

Indian President Ralph Rogers purchased the Torque Manufacturing Company of Plainfield, Connecticut, in 1946. The Torque company had employed G. Briggs Weaver, former Indian chief engineer, to design a line of modular motorcycles, including a 220-cc single, a 440-cc vertical twin, and an 880-cc in-line four. In February, plans were underway to move the Torque Manufacturing Company and another Rogers subsidiary, the Ideal Power Lawn Mower Company, to the Indian plant.

Racing

The 1946 racing calendar was abbreviated—there wasn't even a Daytona event— because there wasn't sufficient lead time after the war ended to marshal the needed riders and resources. Sport Scout riders Ed Kretz and Johnny

Spiegelhoff won the year's two most prestigious events, the Laconia 100 and the Langhorne 100, respectively.

Speedsters Frank Chase and Max Bubeck were up to their high-speed antics again, this time at Rosamond Dry Lake (the Army had taken over nearby Muroc Dry Lake to create what is now known as Edwards Air Force Base). From *Motorcyclist* November 1946:

The lake itself is magnificent for this type of event. The hard packed, mud surface seems limitless once you are on the clay. The cracks in the clay were so fine as to be something that can be ignored by all riders. The breezes that can usually spoil any speed trial event held off until eleven o'clock this morning, thus making almost all runs as near perfect as possible. The surface kicks up so little dust that vision was excellent so long as any rider was in range of the human eye, which in most instances was not very long.

Fastest time made today was the Frank Chase-Max Bubeck Indian which pushed up to the 128.57 mark. Bubeck, long holder of the fastest speed in Time Trials, rode the motorcycle over this wonderful surface to keep his laurels for another year. It would be a big error to say he holds them without a lot of effort since there were plenty of motorcycles on the lake today that had been groomed for just one thing—BEAT BUBECK. Walking off with the Glendale Motorcycle Club Trophy (for fastest 80-ci side-valve) were Frank Chase and Max Bubeck. Then to add just one more notch on the handlebars of this superb motorcycle, Bubeck took the Kurten & Spalding Trophy which was put up for a motorcycle versus a "hot rod," in this instance a Ford V-8 but really cut down.

1947

Again, only the Chief was offered. Changes were in the details only, such as the new Indian head front fender light and Indian script on the tanks.

In February, Indian reorganized, with the Atlas Corporation, the Chemical Bank, and the Marine Midland Banks providing financing. In April, Indian offered the Wigwam for sale. In August, the R. B. Rogers Companies were formally merged with Indian. Indian's cousins were the Ideal Lawn Mower Com-

1946 Chief. *For the 1946 season, continuing financial problems caused the Wigwam to eliminate all models but the Chief. Unlike Harley-Davidson, Indian didn't spend all the war years concentrating on motorcycle production, and this weakened the company. Plans were made to reintroduce a postwar Sport Scout, but Indian never did. Restoration by owner Toney Watson.*

pany and the Torque Manufacturing Company. A headline in the *Springfield Daily News* of October 16, 1947, read: "Motorcycle at Lower Price Planned by Indian Company; Will Make Radically-New Product at East Springfield Plant Starting Next Spring." For the fiscal year, production totaled 11,849. Harley-Davidson built 20,000. The Indian production total includes both 1947 and 1948 models sold during the fiscal year.

Competition

Indian started the competition year in grand style, with riders Jack Horn and Bill Huguley winning first and second places in the 100-Mile Daytona Beach National Amateur Championship. (The "term" amateur is misleading because riders in this class were professionals.) The next day, Johnny Spiegelhoff, riding one of the prewar, under-the-table, big-base Sport Scouts, won the Daytona 200 National Championship (expert class).

Overall, however, Indian's slipping racing position was signified by the number of entrants for the 1947 Laconia event, which included 11 Harley-Davidsons compared to seven Indians. Prewar, Indian often had as many, or more, entrants as did Harley-Davidson, especially for events in the Northeast. Further proof of Indian's decline was Ted Edwards second place; his was the only Indian in the top 10. Indian responded to this bad outing the very next day by beginning planning for the 1948 Model 648 Scout.

On May 31, Max Bubeck accomplished the extraordinary feat of winning the tough two-day 500-mile Greenhorn Enduro in the southern California desert and mountains. What made the feat extraordinary was his mount, a 1939 Indian Four. The machine sported several Bubeck modifications, including an oil cooler, extra oil passages drilled in the crankshaft, and Chevrolet valve springs.

1948

The Chief-only lineup again had only a few changes. The most notable were a new gear-driven oil pump, a new instrument panel with a generator light instead of an ammeter, and a new front-drive speedometer. The Stewart Warner 120-mile-per-hour speedometer now had a gray face

1946 Chief and sidecar. The streamlined sidecar was first available for the 1940 season. Restoration by Bollenbach Engineering.

with a red arrow-shaped pointer, like the forthcoming lightweight models.

During 1946 and 1947, registration of two-wheeled motor vehicles had doubled to about 400,000 units, with the bulk of the increase made up of foreign lightweights. Therefore, Rogers and his investors believed Indian would dominate the American motorcycle industry with its new lightweight Arrow singles and Scout vertical twins.

In early 1948, Rogers led a group of Indian executives on a multi-city tour to introduce the new vertical twin Scouts and Arrow singles to Indian dealers. The traveling team passed on their enthusiasm for Indian's future, and during the tour Indian doubled its number of registered dealers from about 450 to about 900.

Rogers Presents the Indian Arrow and Scout

As the Indian President who was promising revolutionary motorcycles and a revolution in American motorcycle marketing, Ralph B. Rogers faced a hard-sell crowd of Indian dealers whose roots reached back to the board-track days of the 1910s. The dealers' view of American motorcycles and American motorcycling was all about tradition and the slow evolution of Indian motorcycles to, in their eyes, a perfected state. Rogers and his

1946 Chief and sidecar. Instead of an external trunk, luggage was stored behind the removable seat.

Ralph Rogers and G. Briggs Weaver

G. Briggs Weaver came to Indian in 1930 from DuPont Motors, where he had been the chief engineer and stylist for the DuPont automobiles. He arrived at about the time Charles B. Franklin left Indian due to ill health, so he had no rival within the management structure. Weaver inherited the good 45-ci Scout, the outdated 78-ci Four, and the underdeveloped 74-ci Chief. Either Weaver or President du Pont or both were impressed by British motorcycle designs that used the engine as a stress-bearing frame member. So Weaver oversaw the design and development of the 30.50-ci Scout Pony, the 45-ci Motoplane, and the 45-ci Sport Scout along British lines. He also was in charge of the unsuc-

1947. On the left, Ralph B. Rogers, on the right, G. Briggs Weaver.

Weaver's biggest contribution to Indian was probably skirted-fender styling. He also introduced rear suspension. Weaver left Indian during WWII to design a modular series of single-, twin-, and four-cylinder machines.

Indian President Ralph B. Rogers was a millionaire industrialist who was successful in several ventures prior to buying Indian in 1945. He was only 36 years old at the time. Rogers's plan was to flood America with a tide of mass-produced, inexpensive, lightweight motorcycles along continental lines. To do so, he bought out the Torque Manufacturing Company of Plainfield, Connecticut, for which Briggs Weaver worked, so Weaver again became Indian's chief engineer. The new light-

cessful 1936 and 1937 upside-down Fours, and the subsequent final update of the Four with inlet-over-exhaust valve layout and cylinders cast in pairs. Other projects under his direction were the Models 640B and 741 military V-twins, and the Model 841 shaft-drive V-twin. The latter model, however, was largely the baby of President E. Paul du Pont, who made a number of the engineering drawings himself.

weight singles and vertical twins were beautifully styled by Weaver, but proved underdeveloped when put in the hands of customers. Weaver left Indian in 1948, and details of his subsequent life are unknown. Rogers's struggle to save Indian is detailed elsewhere; he left Indian in 1950. As of this writing, Ralph B. Rogers is living in Dallas, having made another fortune in the gravel business.

advertising team had to convince the dealers of two things: first, that the new lightweight models were well designed, thoroughly tested, and well built; second, that a vast new and different market would eagerly accept these radically different Indian lightweights.

Before presenting the Indian Arrow and the Indian Scout, I should like to give you a little background on these designs.

These machines were first designed in 1944 by G. Briggs Weaver. Consequently, as you see them today they represent the result of four years of constant design, development and testing.

During these years, no money or effort was spared to compare the design and construction of these machines with every type of motorcycle

both at home and abroad. . . . The cost of this design, development, and testing project exceeded $500,000.

As you see the machines today, they represent a forward step in design, engineering and production which it will probably take others four to seven years to equal.

Before freezing these designs for production, we have very carefully considered questions of price and quality. It was only after a long and careful consideration that it was decided that these machines must represent quality first, and that price must be fair and commensurate with that quality. However, it is important that you understand this—nothing has been spared in the way of quality because of price consideration.

In tooling the machines for production, we have made a tremendous

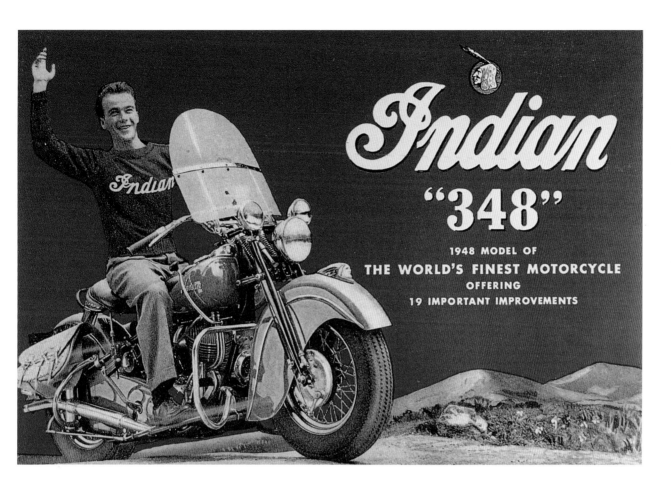

1948 Chief sales catalog. The 1948 Chief's speedometer was driven from the front wheel. From a 1948 advertisement, "You'll never know how much fun motorcycling can be until you ride the new Indian 348. This new Indian gives you all the quality, all the fine construction features, all the strength, power and dependability that earned the title 'World's Finest Motorcycle.'"

1947 Chief and sidecar. An Indian-head light graced the front fender of the 1947 Chief. From a 1947 advertisement, "Pride in possessing, pride in producing . . . a motorcycle that is the last word in elegance and performance. As the '47s start on the way to you riders, Indian's men and women enjoy a gratifying sense of work well done—each knows a feeling of pride in producing the finest motorcycle." Restoration by Jim Sutter; owner: Don Miller.

bet that we would be successful in selling hundreds of thousands of these machines. I can safely say that no motorcycle in the world has ever been tooled to the extent that these new machines are tooled. The dies, patterns, jigs, fixtures and gauges alone have cost $750,000, and we are not through yet.

The same situation exists on plant and machinery. These machines are to be produced in a new plant, engineered solely and wholly for their production. Automatic conveyor lines, rust-proofing installations, the finest painting, baking, and finishing equipment—all brand new—have been purchased and installed specially for these machines.

Actually, the total investment involved in the creation of this new Indian Motocycle Company with its new designs today approximates $6,600,000.

We give you this information so that you will know how seriously management has approached this problem and how confident Indian Management is in the future of the Indian Motocycle Company. Please don't forget, a very substantial portion of the funds invested is the Management's own funds. Please also remember that the active management of the Indian Motocycle Company today is composed of those people who have their own money invested, and are the kind of people who are willing and who do work 12, 14, and 16 hours a day, seven days a week, to make a success of the company.

Rogers admitted his speech was designed as a sales pitch, exactly the sales pitch he thought Indian dealers should give to prospects. Rogers concluded, "If I could know that every one of your prospects and your customers could receive this presentation from you in just this way, I am certain that the Indian dealer organization could sell 100,000 of these machines next year. Good luck!"

Left
1949 Arrow. *Young industrialist Ralph Rogers took over Indian in late 1945 with a plan to market a range of lightweight singles and vertical twins. The single-cylinder Model 149 Arrow was powered by a 13.3-ci overhead-valve engine of about 10 horsepower. Top speed was about 55 miles per hour. Restoration by Bollenbach Engineering.*

Model 149. *Rider's-eye view shows the speedometer with arrow-shaped needle; it was also used on the 1948 Chief.*

Advertising and Sales Promotion

Following Rogers on the dealer convention program was the advertising team. Philip Lukin said:

Beginning today with the showing of these motorcycles, the Indian Company and every Indian dealer has a new sales job. That sales job is to sell Indian Chiefs in greater volume to the dyed-in-the-wool motorcycle rider, the fellow who really likes the finest in heavyweight motorcycles. We also have a second job. We're going to sell our lightweights to those who have always wanted to ride a motorcycle, but who have said, "Those big babies are too much motorcycle for me."

Then we have a third job, and the most important one! We're going to sell the whole American public the idea that motorcycling is great sport and convince them that they want to ride a motorcycle—and that they want to ride an Indian! We're going to do this in two ways. First, we're going to do it by reaching millions and millions of Americans with magazine and newspaper advertising. Second, we're going to reach those who we know are already committed to the idea of riding a motorcycle . . . with direct mail advertising.

In 1948 Indian will spend more money in national advertising than any other motorcycle company.. . .

Lukin then projected pictures of Hollywood's Jane Russell and Allan Ladd, of band leader and crooner Vaughn Monroe, of Notre Dame quarterback Johnny Lujack, of Cleveland Indians pitcher Bob Feller, and others all of whom would appear in upcoming Indian advertisements.

No doubt, the lightweight program looked good on paper. Did Rogers believe all the rosy words offered by himself and his advertising staff, or was this just a typical PR stunt? Rogers was sincere insofar as people believe what they need to believe, and Rogers needed to believe that the money and reputation he had bet on the lightweights was going to pay off. Besides, by this point Rogers's self-serving staff ensured he heard only good news about the lightweight prototypes—a recipe for upcoming disaster.

1949 Arrow. *On the left side were the footshift, kickstarter, and exhaust system. The Arrow and companion Scout vertical twin were the first motorcycles sold in the U.S. with left-side, down-for-low footshift. Describing the Arrow, Indian President Ralph Rogers said, "The Indian Arrow has been designed so that it can stay out in front of traffic. Riders do not have to be afraid of being run over, as is the case with almost all 125 cc machines . . ."*

Lightweight Program Advances . . . and Crashes

In March, G. Briggs Weaver was honored by West Coast Indian dealers for his development of the new lightweight models, the 220-cc Arrow single and the 440-cc Scout vertical twin. Weaver had done his design work as a member of the Torque Manufacturing Company after leaving Indian during the war.

In the spring, Indian began relocating machinery and people from the Wigwam to the new East Springfield one-story plant. The new vertical twins and singles weren't ready in time for the all-important spring sales season, due largely to the same problems with suppliers that had plagued Chief production. In May, Indian laid off 600 workers, drawing the factory roll down from 1,650 to 1,050. In the summer, when ordinarily production would start to ramp up on the next year's models, the decision was made

not to offer a 1949-model Chief. This action was taken because of a number of production problems that plagued Arrow and Scout deliveries.

In July, the first vertical-twin Scouts and Arrow singles were offered for sale from the company owned store in Springfield. Meanwhile, about a half-year's worth of production effort—late 1947 and early 1948—was spent on the 1948-model Chief.

Then, catastrophe struck. The few Arrows and Scouts that were delivered weren't reliable when given the rawhide treatment by experienced Indian riders. Solving the production and reliability problems required additional financing, and the financial aspect occupied much of President Ralph Rogers' time.

There were several problems with the Torque-designed Arrow and Scout. There was no provision for adjusting the primary drive chain, which Indian excused by calling it a "pre-stretched" chain. My goodness, why didn't

Indian and Harley-Davidson think of that before! Probably because there is no such thing.

Crankcases were likely to fill with oil when the motorcycles weren't ridden for several days. Dealer's were advised to seat the oil check valve between the oil tank and the oil pump by using a hammer and punch on the valve! Engine tune-up specifications hadn't been thoroughly worked out before production, resulting in rough low-speed running. In answer to complaints, the factory sent out new settings for the spark-plug gap, the magneto point gap, and the valve clearances.

Most distressing of all reported problems was hard starting. Mild-mannered men were apt to use sailor language before the starting drill was finished. Some imagined wistfully how nice it would be to live atop a long, steep hill, thus simplifying starting. The main culprit was the small magneto, which was adequate for the single-cylinder Arrow but not strong enough to handle the additional load of a distributor in the twin-cylinder Scout. According to road tester Jimmy Hill, the faulty magneto was a lower-cost replacement for a pre-production unit that had worked properly.

Poor starting was also the result of carburetor choke leaks. This problem was addressed by instructing the dealers to seal off air sources with solder, cork, and shellac, and to modify the choke disc with saw cuts and pliers—a quick and crude response at best.

Then there were problems that had nothing to do with the design. To design a motorcycle is one thing. To comply with the design is another. Arrows and Scouts were leaving the factory without conforming to design specifications. The first 1,660 Arrows and 268 Scouts left without the wheel hubs greased. After taking corrective action at the factory, the same problem resurfaced in Scouts serial numbered 2,000 through 2,047! Some Arrows were shipped without removing the welding flux and acid from the gas and oil tanks. This was serious stuff, as rust in the oil tank could clog up oil passages. Telescopic forks leaked because they were assembled without cleaning the sealing surfaces. Dealers had to partially disassemble the forks, clean them, and reinstall gaskets.

Plainly, production had gone to hell. A major problem was a lack of quality control by subcontractors. In the postwar boom, suppliers were not intimidated by the risk of losing the relatively small business offered by the Indian Company. Desperate to break up production jams, Indian quality inspectors began overlooking problems that they reasoned could be later fixed by the dealers.

Very noisy valvetrains on some units was caused by mismatching of drive gears. The gears were made in two different styles, the difference being the pitch angle, a measurement of the geometrical relationship between engaging gears. Early Arrows had cam gears with a 20-degree pitch angle, and later Arrows had a 14-1/2-degree pitch angle. Although the two types of gears had different part numbers and were shipped in separate boxes properly marked, the part numbers weren't marked on the gears. The later 14-1/2-degree gears were cadmium plated and the earlier 20-degree gears weren't, but the cadmium plating became less obvious after the gears had been in use. Lack of good factory records resulted in a haphazard application process. Most singles between serial numbers 1001 and 3485 needed 20-degree teeth, but a few were supplied with 14-1/2-degree teeth. Nearly all twins had the 20-degree teeth gears, but some were fitted with the other gears. Evidently, mismatching was occurring in the dealerships, because the factory had to issue instructions. Mechanics were told to place a 1/16-inch diameter drill between the teeth of a gear. If the bit could be rocked between the gear teeth, it was a late 14-1/2-degree gear. If the drill fit tightly, it was an early 20-degree gear.

Valvetrain noise could also be the result of improper gear installation. The valvetrain gears were supported by predrilled plain bearings. Sometimes, the internal diameters of the bearings were distorted when the bearings were pressed into the cases. This was solved in late 1948 by precision boring the bearings after they had been pressed in.

Roughly 3,000 1948 Chiefs—a mere quarter of the 1947 Chief production—kept the dealers in business while waiting for the promised lightweights. In August, the new East Springfield plant officially opened. The plant, however, wasn't automated to the degree that had been originally planned. The September *Business Week* published an article about Indian's postwar program. Things looked rosy indeed. But also in September, at about the time that the solutions appeared at hand for the production and reliability problems of the Arrow and Scout, Rogers' projected lightweight revolution was given the death sentence by the British government's devaluation of the Pound Sterling from about $4 to about $3. This had the effect of lowering the price of the growing body of imported British motorcycles by about one-third. At the stroke of a pen, Indian's pricing went from competitive to uncompetitive. In November, Indian released another 250 employees, leaving about 800 in the force. Employment was thus about half what had been projected as required to bring the new lineup of singles and vertical twins to market.

1948 Competition

The Sport Scout had been out of production since 1942, so spare parts were beginning to be a problem. Meanwhile, Harley-Davidson had released a relative flood of WR and WRTT racers. Harley-Davidson's book *The Legend Begins* lumps all the 45-ci racers under the WR family tree and lists production figures as 100 in 1946, 20 in 1947, and 292 in 1948. These racing Harleys benefited from a continuous development program in contrast to the nearly extinct Sport Scout.

To counterattack, Indian launched the 1948 Model 648 Scout. The effort produced a combination of complete motorcycles and uninstalled powerplants, totaling 50 units. The Model 648, or big-base Scout in common

1949 Scout. *The 1949 Scout weighed about 315 pounds fully serviced. The red saddlebags of this unrestored example are either a period aftermarket item or a lower-cost alternative set not publicized in Indian literature. Regular Indian saddlebags were black leather.*

1949 Scout. *The Model 249 Scout was a double-up of the Arrow. The two-cylinder vertical twin displaced 26.6 ci. Top speed was about 85 miles per hour. Comparing the Scout to the Arrow, Indian President Rogers said, "The Scout, of course, has the advantage of flashing performance and speed, as well as the superior deluxe comfort which comes from the combination of the aircraft-type hydraulic front fork and the latest spring frame rear springing."*

description, featured the big crankcases pioneered just before the war, an aluminum gear-type oil pump, and Model 841 flywheels.

There were an estimated 500 different parts used in the Model 648, of which all but 10 were standard parts. Of the standard parts, 65 were already on back order to fill existing orders and 420 parts were in stock. The estimated cost of the standard parts was $340 per motorcycle. The special parts situation was different. Here, the estimated cost was $365 per motorcycle. The net result was that Indian had to underwrite the cost—sell the motorcycles at a loss—to the tune of $400 per motorcycle. All of this effort was possible under the banner of advertising, and only a $20,000 net direct motorcycle cost was allotted to the program. This was a puny outlay compared to the millions being spent on the development of the new lightweights.

The Model 648 program garnered the best possible payoff with Floyd Emde winning the 1948 Daytona 200 at a record pace of 84.1 miles per hour. Still, the starting lineup of the Daytona 200 gave evidence of the changing balance of power in American racing. Taking 1939 as a typical prewar year, the breakdown of the 47 finishers showed Harley-Davidson at 48 percent, Indian at 36 percent, and all others at 16 percent. In 1948, the competing marques finishing were Harley-Davidson 51 percent, Indian 25 percent, and all others 25 percent. Except for a solitary BMW, all "others" were British motorcycles. Harley-Davidson was holding its own, but Indian was slipping.

1949: The Arrow and Scout Models

Although the lightweight marketing program had begun in the summer of 1948, the new motorcycles were 1949 models. The Arrow single and Scout

vertical twin each had a bore and stroke of 2-3/8x3 inches, yielding displacements of 220 cc for the Arrow and 440 cc for the Scout. Power outputs from these mildly tuned engines were about 10 and 20 horsepower respectively. With dry weights of but 245 and 280 pounds, acceleration was competitive with 500-cc British machines. The single would top at about 55 miles per hour, and the twin would run about 85 miles per hour, about the same as 500-cc British bikes. The engine layout of the Scout included pushrod tubes angled away from the cylinder bore and a single carburetor. Would-be speed merchants were handicapped because on the inlet side the close proximity of the pushrod tubes prevented an effective twin-carb modification. Advertised paint choices were Brilliant Red, Seafoam Blue, Sunshine Yellow, and Turquoise. The dominant color was also featured on the fenders, brake drum, fork, speedometer housing, fuel tank, oil tank, and chain guard. The headlight shell was black.

Racing 1949: A Bad Year

At Daytona, Indian's share of the top 20 places were Ted Edwards's seventh place, Walter Troxel's 14th, and Earl Givens's 20th. Kretz, as usual, was a factor early in the race, running second on his Sport Scout for a number of laps before his motorcycle failed. Kretz's fastest lap was 2 minutes, 47.87 seconds, while Norton-mounted winner Dick Klamfoth's fastest lap was a mere 0.52 seconds quicker. Evidently, the design work on the big-base Scout hadn't been followed up by the continuous development seen in Harley-Davidson's WR 45s and Norton's 500-cc Manx.

Indian entered 12 prototype 498-cc vertical twin Warriors at Laconia in June, all saddled by factory-sponsored riders. The Warrior was an enlarged Model

Prototype Torque Four. *Working for the Torque Manufacturing Company of Plainfield, Connecticut, former Indian engineer G. Briggs Weaver developed a modular lineup of a single, a twin, and this four-cylinder model. Major engine components such as cylinders and cylinder heads were shared by all models. Ralph Rogers bought the Torque company and planned to market the full modular range, but the four-cylinder model never reached production. Owner: Dr. John Patt.*

Prototype Torque Four. *The Torque cylinder head design maximized the exposure of cylinder head area into the air stream. Most likely this is a 42-ci engine because it is known that the original design displacement for the twin-cylinder Scout was 21 ci. The right footboard is missing.*

Max Bubeck, Frank Chase, and Pop Shunk

Shortly before the 1948 Rosamond trials, Frank Chase and Max Bubeck put twin carburetors and a four-lobe cam setup on their Chout. By equipping each of the two cams with two half-width lobes in lieu of the former single wide lobe, more precise valve timing was achieved. Famed Indian tuner "Pop" Shunk lent a hand in these modifications, and Frank Chase spent many hours experimenting with the two-carb porting. All intermediate gears in the transmission were removed, as well as the kickstarter and the gearshift lever. In place of the latter, a stub lever was mounted directly on the gearbox in order to locate neutral. The foot clutch was replaced by a hand clutch.

On June 27, at Rosamond Dry Lake, about 100 miles north of Los Angeles, the team of Frank Chase, Max Bubeck, and Pop Shunk entered the high-speed trials of the Glendale Motorcycle Club. Jockey Bubeck rode the Chout. Going head to head against Bubeck was Bus Schaller on a Harley-Davidson 80-ci overhead-valve.

Bumblebees, so the old yarn goes, don't know that theoretically they can't fly, hence, they go about the business of flying. Chase and Bubeck were like bumblebees. They should have known that, all things being equal, a side-valve 80-ci Indian Chief can't outrun an 80-ci overhead-valve Harley-Davidson big twin. Perhaps the Indian duo simply knew that all things are seldom equal.

Steve Stevens was piloting the Bus Schaller-prepared Harley-Davidson big twin. Stevens was one of the first riders through the trap, and turned 130 miles per hour. Bubeck and Chase weren't dismayed, for their Chout harbored yet another new trick. Following the lead of their friend Chuck Bryant, who'd pushed the urge of his stroker Chief from 58 to 67 horsepower, Bubeck and Chase had installed an oxygen bottle and regulator. Bubeck's first two runs netted a disappointing 118 and 119 miles per hour because the ignition timing had somehow been too far advanced. Max confirmed the problem on the second run near the end of the course, when manually retarding the ignition timing resulted in higher revolutions.

Steve Stevens countered with a disappointing 120-mile-per-hour trip, a result of miscalculating gear ratios when changing sprockets after the first run. Bubeck retorted with 133.82 miles per hour on the Chout. Stevens and Schaller then got the Harley set right and upped the ante to 134.32 miles per hour. Amazingly, Bubeck's next run was exactly the same, 134.32 miles per hour.

Bubeck started his fifth run: "Then it was feeling right. I knew it. It was strong, no pinging or anything. And then we ran up to a 134.12, the exact same speed that Bus Schaller's Harley-Davidson ran through there. Of course, by then we were all gung-ho. Everything was still right and it was still fairly early in the day and the

1948. Left to right: Frank Chase, Max Bubeck, and Pop Shunk. They stand proudly behind the all-time fastest unstreamlined Indian, clocked at over 135 miles per hour.

wind hadn't come up. So I thought, I'll just fool around a little more and feel it out. I just loafed on down the track until the trap came in sight, and I got on it. I went up to 4600 [rpm], a 135.58." Two subsequent runs were slower because a cross wind developed and steadily warming air meant less efficient combustion.

"We'd made one concession," Bubeck continued.

We had left the sidestand on, so we didn't have to worry about where in the hell to park it. I came back after the 135.5 run, came back by the timing stand, and I set the thing over on the sidestand. Of course, with no kickstarter, I left it idling. It was sitting there, idling at about 550 or 600 rpm, going chunka, chunka, chunka, chunka. I went over to get my time. When I came back, I could hardly find the machine, there were so many people around it. There was a little short lever down on the gearshift. I pulled the right-hand clutch in, reached over on the right side and snapped the thing in gear, and then I just feathered the clutch and took off, and chugged on back down the lake.

Incidentally, Bubeck didn't use the oxygen bottle.

No one could have known that this day they had seen the *all time fastest unstreamlined Indian*: 135.58 miles per hour. The Harley-Davidson favorites never bettered 134.12 miles per hour. Poor Bus Schaller, Steve Stevens, and the Harley-Davidson fans. They'd been well and truly stung by the Indian bumblebee.

Circa 1946 hotrod bike. *The author's 1938 Four is restored to circa-1946 custom specifications as a Max Bubeck replica. The Vard forks were available in 1946 from the Pasadena, California, company. Other modifications include a top-side oil pressure gauge that can be easily read while on the run and a down-turned exhaust pipe to permit larger saddlebags. The front fender is a Bob Stark idea and actually used to be a Royal Enfield rear fender. Bubeck designed and assembled the replica, and coordinated all outsourced work. Major services were provided by Ken Young and Son, Indian Motor Works, Starklite Cycle, and Mike Parti.*

249 Scout, thus with roots outside Indian. There was nothing in Indian's considerable side-valve racing expertise that could help them with the Warrior. By switching to overhead-valve racing, the Indian factory threw away all the hard-won advantages of 30 years of trial-and-error side-valve development. The factory staff had been side-valve experts; they were now overhead-valve beginners.

Laconia's mile-long circuit of hills and hairpins put less emphasis on speed than on acceleration and handling. This was fortunate, as Ed Kretz reported that the maximum speed of the 498-cc Warriors at the 1949 Laconia was only about 100 miles per hour (Kretz's Sport Scout was capable of 115 miles per hour at Daytona). Kretz did credit the vertical twin Warrior's acceleration with being on par with his V-twin Sport Scout. In any case,

speed wasn't a factor in Indian's sorry 1949 Laconia outing.

The problem was reliability—specifically the lack thereof. The monumental flaw that felled all 12 factory-sponsored Warriors was an unreliable Edison-Splitdorf magneto. The company had built Indian's magnetos for a generation. Tens of thousands had demonstrated reliability, the most recent of which was the magneto used on the Model 648 Scout. Yet, incredibly, all 12 factory-sponsored Warriors suffered magneto failure.

Bailing a Sinking Ship

Despite the crippling blow of 1948's British money devaluation, Rogers was determined to make every possible effort to save the new light-

Max Bubeck and his historic dirt flyers. *The black and white bike is Max's 1939 Four which he campaigned in southern California enduros from 1939 through 1948, winning the famous Greenhorn Enduro in 1947. The blue motorcycle is Max's 1949 Scout, his enduro ride from 1949 through 1969. The engine was enlarged to 30.50 ci in 1949. Max built the swinging arm rear suspension in 1955, and won the famous Green Horn Enduro in 1962.*

weights, as the entire future of Indian had already been gambled on these machines. With the large debt already owed by Indian, there could be no question of putting the lightweights aside to spend nonexistent dollars updating the lineup with a totally new Chief and Sport Scout.

Rogers was creative. In January 1949, Indian arranged for the Vincent-HRD Company of England to fabricate a prototype Indian-Vincent, consisting of a 1000-cc Vincent overhead-valve V-twin motor mounted in a 1948 Chief chassis. This hybrid was a potential 1950-model that would be continued two or three years until a new four-cylinder Indian could be prepared for the market. While the idea looked like a winner, the Vincent company was coping with their own considerable financial problems, which likely precluded an engineering tie-up between the two companies. Meanwhile, Indian's contract for CZ 125-cc two-stroke motorcycles had expired, and Indian was faced with a lack of light-weight motorcycles before CZ deliveries could be resumed.

In April 1949, to gain time and additional capital Rogers traveled to England and cut a financial deal with J. Brockhouse & Company, Ltd. Rogers secured a $1.5 million loan from Brockhouse in exchange for seating John Brockhouse on the board of directors and allowing the Brockhouse firm to set up and manage an independent distributing company, Indian Sales Corporation. Under the arrangement, the Indian Motocycle Company agreed to build new Indians and to sell them exclusively to Indian Sales, at specified prices. Indian Sales retained the exclusive Indian distribution rights so long as they ordered minimum specified quantities of new Indians.

In November 1949, Rogers agreed to let Indian Sales Corporation distribute the following British motorcycles in the United States: AJS, Douglas, Excelsior (no connection with the former American marque), Matchless (except in California), Norton, Royal Enfield, and Vincent.

Indian suffered a great blow in 1949 when Hap Alzina purchased the right to distribute BSA motorcycles in the 11 western states. Indian was already finding it difficult to hold on to dealers because of Arrow and Scout reliability problems. As Alzina had been Indian's most successful distributor, his move was a serious psychological blow to Springfield and no doubt influenced more dealers and racers to abandon Indian's sinking ship. The growing number of Indian deserters left behind loyalists who could not face reality or those who had not yet found a better deal. Ed Kretz was in neither category. The man whose racing career had been synonymous with Indian would switch his racing support to Triumph in 1950.

Countdown to Failure

1950–1962

Rogers' Indian Motocycle Company decided to continue building Arrows and Scouts through the end of February 1950 at the rate of 250 motorcycles per month, and to mark these models down 25 percent—meaning a loss on each machine sold—in order to increase operating capital and hopefully pull Indian up by its bootstraps. Headlining the 1950 program were new vertical twin 500cc Warriors and Warrior TTs, the latter an off-road model designed specifically for American TT racing and enduros.

At this point, somewhere between 8,000 and 15,000 of the new lightweight models had been built. This was far below the planned production level, which in turn drove up the cost of the Arrows and Scouts because fewer new motorcycles were available to share the distribution of fixed overhead costs. Due to the reliability problems discussed earlier, a considerable number of 1949 Arrows and Scouts were on hand in dealerships as the 1950

1953 Chief. Here we see the black generator belt guard, a feature of 1940–1942 and 1950–1953 Chiefs. The 1946–1948 Chiefs had the guard the same color as the tanks, fenders, and chain guard. Notice the sidestand angle and length, which were made to work with the center stand. By leaning the motorcycle to the left, the bike can be balanced on the front wheel and sidestand. Then the center stand can be lowered, and the motorcycle allowed to rock up on the center stand. This is an easy job for a 90-pound weakling, and a tremendous kick to accomplish in front of Gold Wing riders.

model year was about to begin. Dealers were advised to mark down these machines and to clear stocks so the factory could deliver new 1950 models.

Sales of the 1950 models weren't sufficient to instill confidence to the lending banks, so despite his extraordinary efforts, Ralph Rogers' presidency was doomed. Behind the scenes, John Brockhouse had been working hard to convince the Indian Motocycle Company's major creditors that a management change was needed. Brockhouse completed the coup at the January 1950 board meeting and replaced Rogers as president.

Rogers has been derided over the years by Indian fans, but this is more an emotional reaction than a fair assessment. Rogers' lightweight motorcycle plan was a good idea—consider the plan of attack made clear at the 1948 dealer conventions. In fact, the lightweight marketing program was remarkably similar to the invasion Honda would mount a decade later. One could be cruelly concise and conclude the lightweight idea was better than the lightweight motorcycles. Although that was the truth, it was not the whole truth. The fall of the lightweights had as much to do with British financial policy as it did with Indian deficiencies. Rogers spent a lot of his own money, effort, and emotion on the Indian venture. Rogers' predecessor, E. Paul du Pont and his brother Francis, were financial wizards with the right contacts, yet they had only mixed financial success with Indian, roughly breaking even in their 15-year financial roller-coaster ride. Besides, in the absence of Rogers' lightweight, Indian was no more than an even bet to survive the turbulent postwar industrial era with its old V-twin strategy.

1953 Chief. *The headlight panel was brought out in 1952, and like the engine cowling, it has been adapted to many 1950 and 1951 restored Chiefs. Telescopic forks have also been used on lots of 1946 through 1948 Chiefs. In fact, stock 1950 and 1951 Chiefs are rarely seen. The 1952 and 1953 bench saddle was more comfortable for the rider when riding double than the old spring-suspended saddle. The old saddle carried the rider on the essentially unsprung and thinly padded nose. Turquoise was a standard Indian color for 1952 and 1953. Restoration by Starklite Cycle.*

In September 1950, E. Paul du Pont died. Many, perhaps most, Americans have a strange notion that rich people get that way only by being lucky or by being crooks. It seldom occurs to Joe Average that brains and drive are more likely attributes of the rich. E. Paul du Pont was a shrewd investor, a talented engineer, and a strong manager. Today, we should be grateful to him for rescuing Indian at the point of impending collapse in 1930. Quite likely, without E. Paul du Pont there would have been no post-1930 Indians. Without du Pont, any post-1930 Indians would have been built without G. Briggs Weaver, the stylist and engineer E. Paul du Pont brought from DuPont Motors. Think of it—without E. Paul du Pont there would have been no classic open-fender models of the late 1930s and no skirted-fender models.

1950 Model Changes and Racing Decline

On the Chief, the headline features were the new telescopic front fork and the 80-ci (1300-cc) engine. The added displacement was achieved by changing the stroke from 4-7/16 inches to 4-13/16 inches; the bore remained 3-1/4 inches. The front fender had a shorter front section and a smaller skirt. To account for the taller parking stance resulting from the telescopic fork, the sidestand mounting angle was changed. A Raceway air cleaner was standard. On the forward part of the primary-drive cover was a bulge necessitated by the new engine shock absorber.

Leftover Arrows and Scouts were marketed as 1950 models. These had black frames instead of frames painted to match the tanks and fenders. The

Indian Celebrities

Among President Ralph Rogers' bag of tricks was a massive publicity campaign for the forthcoming lightweight models. He hired the prestigious advertising agency of Lawrence Fertig & Company, Inc. The agency photographed and received testimonials from Hollywood's Alan Ladd, John Payne, Robert Ryan, and Jane Russell. Star athletes used in Indian advertisements were Cleveland Indians pitcher Bob Feller, Notre Dame quarterback Johnny Lujack, tennis champion Bobby Riggs, and Los Angeles Rams quarterback Bob Waterfield. Nationally broadcast radio sportscaster Bill Stern, sort of the Howard Cosell of the era, endorsed riding the new Indians with a pitch that empha-

Husband and wife, Bob Waterfield and Jane Russell. Waterfield was the quarterback of the Los Angeles Rams, then the city's only major sports team. Russell was the latest Hollywood sex symbol.

sized how easy it was to learn to ride. He even made the claim that motorcycling was safer than riding in a car and backed this up with statistics. Band leader, crooner, and radio star Vaughn Monroe also appeared in the ad campaign. Monroe differed from the rest in that he was really an Indian enthusiast. These personalities were considered important in recruiting the nonriding public into motorcycling.

To impress prospects who were already motorcyclists, racing stars gave testimonials. These included Ed Kretz, Ted Edwards, and Johnny Spiegelhoff. Even old Cannonball Baker was used in some publicity photos.

The all-out marketing assault included full-page advertisements in five farming magazines with a combined monthly circulation of 21 million. Full-page ads also ran in *Mechanix Illustrated*, *Popular Mechanics*, and *Popular Science*. *Colliers*, *Varsity*, *Esquire*, and *Argosy*, all men's magazines, had Indian ads. *Indian News,* a 6-inch by 9-inch magazine with a black and white cover except for a red title area, was replaced by *Indian* magazine, an 8-1/2 by 11-1/2-inch magazine with a full-color cover. The aim was to reach an estimated 400,000 prospects for the Indian lightweights. Half of these prospects already rode small machines such as Whizzer and Servi-Cycle motorbikes, Cushman motorscooters, and so on. The Indian advertising effort was the largest motorcycle ad campaign that had ever been tried to that time.

new Warrior and Warrior TT had distinctive tank decals plus a black frame and oil tank. On all Torque models, the horn was mounted low in front of the engine; this was also true on late-1949 models.

Indian's sales decline was matched by a plummet in racing success. No national titles fell to Indian in 1950. With the selling prices of Indian vertical twins well above those of British brands sold by Indian dealers, what little racing support that could be generated was to the benefit of the British marques, primarily Norton.

Canadian Billy Mathews won the 1950 Daytona 200 on a Norton. The sweater he wore for publicity shots gave equal billing to the Indian Sales and Norton logos, but that was the closest Indian came to glory in the national circuit.

1951–1953 Changes

Some 1951 Chiefs were fitted with a rear-drive, 110-mile-per-hour Corbin speedometer with a black face and white lettering, while others used the front-drive Stewart Warner speedometer as in 1948 and 1950. The 1951 Warrior had a two-color paint scheme on the tank and a new tank decal. A Brockhouse-built, side-valve 250-cc single named the "Brave" was imported.

The 1952 range consisted of the Chief, the Warrior TT, and the Brave. About eight prototype 1952 Warrior road models were assembled, but true production wasn't undertaken. The Chief had a new, more abbreviated front fender, a fork shield, a footboard-mounted dimmer switch, an engine cowling, and a low-mounted Torque muffler. John Bull rubber tie-down straps were used in lieu of some clips.

Max Bubeck: Indian Diehard

Diehards such as Max Bubeck always did their bit to keep Indian in the news. To this end, Bubeck entered the Cactus Derby, a 458-mile desert run in southern California that started at midnight.

Bubeck still knows the southern California desert like you know your backyard. I think he could be parachuted blindfolded into any place in the Mojave Desert, and he would instantly know where he was within a mile. Here's his account of his ride in the 1950 Cactus Derby:

Again in 1950, I had a lighting problem. And 10 minutes after I left Riverside I didn't have any lights. Frank Chase was riding with me, and he was riding a Chout. The Chout, believe it or not, didn't have a battery in it. It had a German Bosch generator that at idle would put out good light. It had such a fantastic voltage regulator that you didn't need a battery, except [chuckle] if you got riding on a fire road and come up to a quick corner and hit the brakes and locked up the rear wheel, well, then the engine died—you got no lights at all, and it gets very dark. But anyway, between us we managed to ride side-by-side most of the time, and I could utilize his lights. But then, just before daylight we got into a real miserable canyon leading out of Lucerne Valley and going over into the area that's now called the Newbury Springs area.

Frank took off and left me, and I would have to literally stop until the next rider would come along. And the minute the lights showed, I'd start riding again. Then it was starting to get grayish dawn; we finally got out of the canyon, and it wasn't all that bad. I could go a little faster, but I was still just poking along because everything was about the same color, the rocks and bushes and everything else. Finally, I got pretty

Max Bubeck and vertical twin, 1950. Bubeck is a diehard Indian man.

well adjusted to the light, and I started moving quicker.

I could see the highway down, oh, three or four miles ahead and see the car lights going along. I thought, well, if I can get to that highway—because I knew where we were going to go—well, when I get to the highway I can make up time again. This, again, was still back in the days when it was 24 miles an hour all the time, so I wasn't all that late. I was maybe five or six minutes late, but I knew we had about eight miles of highway to even things up on, so I kept going faster and faster. By the time I got to the highway it was almost halfway decent visibility, and so when I got to the highway I just laid down on that motorcycle and turned it on. Guys at the check said they could hear me coming the last five miles [chuckle]. It must have been turning about 8,000 or something [laughter]—just left it on, and got there, just did get in on time. So I didn't lose any points.

After that, it was great. My speedometer was *spot on* with whoever had laid out the run. I was working right and my machine was working right. We had a miserable [time]; it was by far the roughest Cactus Derby we'd ever been on. We left Newbury, and then we went east a little further, and then we turned northeast, across by the power lines that came out of the Hoover Dam area. We went along them for about two or three miles and then we got over in the area that's known as the Devil's Playground. That's where the Union Pacific goes from Barstow to Vegas. It's the sink hole of the Mojave River. It was *endless* sand and crap.

Coming into Kelso, we came through the so-called town dump. Back in those days, they'd just go out a couple of hundred yards and dump all their crap. It just looked like an old smelter or something there were so many rusty tin cans and crap [out there]. I mean, they just dumped it out there. Well, the road went right through this little dump for Kelso.

A guy by the name of Huck Koosan, riding a Matchless, had won the 1949 run, when I had gotten fourth. Just before I got into Kelso, here's Huck sitting there, alongside his Matchless, and he's got his pliers and his diagonals out. And he must have 200 yards of barbed wire wrapped up in his rear wheel. It looked almost like a disc wheel, you know. He caught a hunk of this and he kept going until it finally came to a screeching halt. I said, "Aw geez, what a mess that is, Huck!" And he says, "Well, it's your run from here on. It looks like I'm through."

We finally got to the Union Pacific tracks and the little section there called Kelso. That's where the check was, and I was there on time. Luckily, I saw there was a Union Pacific freight sitting there. After the check, we had to cross the tracks—and this is uphill—the freight was headed uphill. The course just went right across the tracks, and there was no crossroad there, I mean where the check was. Those big, high mainline rails are about eight inches tall (chuckle), and I bounced across and banged the frame on 'em and everything, and I *just did* get across about 50 feet before the locomotive [chuckle]. From then on, we went on a nice graded dirt road all the way to the next check.

We went into the next check and then we cut out across the dry lake and across a lot of miserable uphill sand. And I mean *miserable* because there were a lot of guys that were just having a helluva time. In fact, Ralph Adams and a few other guys were struggling through there, and he was a good rider. I kept on slugging away.

See, we didn't have a . . . well, we had the equipment, I guess, as much as you had in later years, except a lot of guys now use knobbies. I never did; I always used the trials universal. I still felt that I got, by using low air pressure and screwing the tires to the rim, I felt that I got as good or better traction, in sand especially, than you did with the knobbies. Anyway, the sand was just blow-drift sand, and certain textures of sand you just don't get the traction.

A lot of us had a lot of struggle, but we made it and got into Twenty-Nine Palms. From Twenty-Nine Palms we went over toward Joshua Valley, and from Joshua we went on up into Big Bear, and went right on up past Big Bear and then cut down an old fire road and back down through Redlands and Colton, and back into Riverside.

Huck Koosan's words were kind of prophetic, because I did go on to win the run. It was 458 miles in one day, and I lost a total of three points, and rode all night with no lights!

Indian Racing Fights Back

In the early part of 1951, racing wins didn't happen for Indian riders—that was the new definition of normalcy. In February, the Daytona 100-Mile Amateur Class had only 10 Indians compared to 44 Harley-Davidsons and 58 British motorcycles. Dick Klamfoth won the Daytona 200-miler on a Norton, gathering glory for Indian Sales but not for Indian motorcycles.

By June there were still no Indian national titles. Glory was recaptured briefly on June 17 at Freemansburg, Pennsylvania, when the grand old man of hillclimbing, 54-year-old Howard Mitzell, won the main event on an Indian 61-ci twin.

Another sweet victory was Joe Gee's Warrior TT-mounted win of the 1951 Jack Pine Enduro. This off-road event was a favorite of Harley-Davidson riders, who had won a string of 17 consecutive Jack Pines from 1925 through 1942.

Most amazing of all though was the rise of a new Indian "wrecking crew" from the ashes of Indian's former greatness.

To give an assessment of the Indian Wrecking Crew, we turn to Tom Sifton. But first, an introduction. Sifton was held in awe, as evidenced by the titles of articles appearing now and then in *Cycle* magazine. In November 1950 there was "Tom Sifton, Sovereign of Harley-Davidson Speed," and in September 1951 there was "Sifton Harleys Sweep Bay Meadows." In recalling those days, Sifton said that three Indian builders had more speed in their Sport Scouts than the Sifton Harley-Davidsons during late 1951 and all of 1952 and 1953.

Three superlative Indian Sport Scout racers had indeed been built by Dick Gross, Art Hafer, and the combined efforts of Bill Tuman and Erwin "Smitty" Smith. These Sport Scouts were ridden respectively by Bobby Hill, Ernie Beckman, and Bill Tuman. These riders all rode Norton overhead-cam singles in road races, but preferred the handling and the broad power band of the Sport Scout for flat tracking. Girder forks, rigid frames, and hand-shifted three-speed transmissions weren't handicaps in flat tracking. Bucking the trend of former Indian riders deserting for British bikes, this trio carried on with zero factory support and only occasional dealer help.

The Dick Gross-prepared bike ridden by Bobby Hill was the most radical of the new Indian Wrecking Crew. The most extreme of Gross's modifications was the use of ball bearings on both ends of the mainshaft as well as in the connecting rod big ends, his goal, undoubtedly, to reduce friction. The ball-bearing setup required machining away considerable connecting rod metal, a drawback in terms of reliability.

Gross also built a mile-track motorcycle for Hill that used a four-cam valve gear. In the four-cammer, there were two half-width lobes on each cam instead of one full-width lobe. Special cam followers, or valve lifters, were

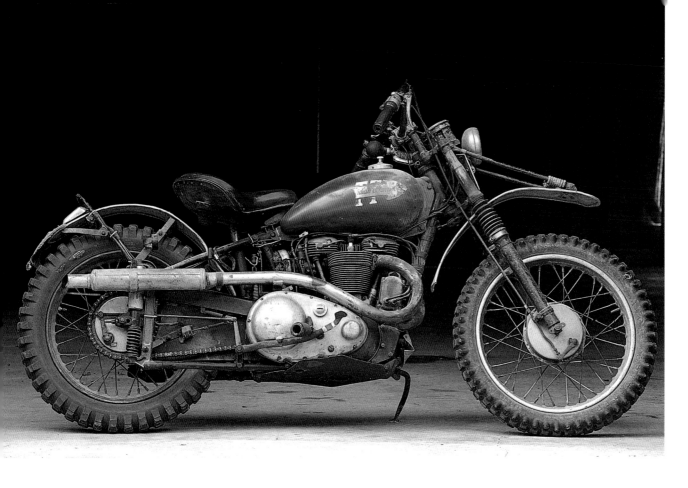

1950–1952 Warrior TT. This banged-up Warrior TT gives evidence by its replacement fenders that it was used after Indian built their last vertical twins, the 1952 Warrior TTs. Another modification is the Chief saddle. Owner: Don Miller.

Below
1950–1952 Warrior TT. Although the factory name was "Warrior TT," the common name of these machines became "TT Warrior." Right out of the box, without the necessity of removing lights, these were highly competitive motorcycles in TT racing—short courses that favored handling and acceleration over top speed. The Warrior TT was also very successful as an enduro mount, with rider Joe Gee winning the prestigious Jack Pine enduro in 1951. Owner Bob Shingler checks gas prior to firing up his pride and joy.

1950 Warrior road racer. This Warrior road racer is from the Shingler racing stable of mounts used in current historic motorcycle racing. This example is in 1949 Laconia trim; note the large rectangular oil tank. Indian ran 12 such vertical twins in the 1949 Laconia 100-Mile National Championship road race, but all 12 expired with magneto failure. Restored by owner Bob Shingler.

The Last Scalp

On October 11, 1953, a race that should have been part of the past summer, but which had been rained out, provided an encore for both racing and sunny skies. At Williams Grove, Pennsylvania, the Eight-Mile National Championship was run on the half-mile oval. The day was all so ordinary. The ordinary parking lot was dominated by Harley-Davidsons, Triumphs, and BSAs. Less than one in 20 motorcycles was an Indian, as the firm had been in only token production for the past several years.

In the main event, Bobby Hill and his Sport Scout got the best start, followed by Buck Brigance on a Harley-Davidson KR, and Ernie Beckman on a Sport Scout. In the third turn, Brigance got in trouble and Dick Klamfoth and his Norton single eased by. The order of Hill, Beckman, and Klamfoth continued until the ninth lap, when Hill slid wide in the corner and Beckman took the lead. That was the way this typical 1953 flat-track national concluded. The finishing order was Beckman, Hill, and Klam-

Ernie Beckman wins the last national racing championship on an Indian.

foth, or for brand watchers, Indian, Indian, and Norton.

The race, well, it was just another race. Back in Milwaukee, Harley-Davidson staffer David H. Warren had the job of writing the intercompany letter describing the event to key factory personnel. Of the day's races, Warren wrote:

"The expert consolation was where the best race of the day was. The people stood and cheered this more than they did the national . . ."

History is like that, meaning you can't always tell what's important until much later. The people who cheered loudest for the expert consolation could not know that on October 11, 1953, at Williams Grove, Pennsylvania, Indian had collected its last national racing championship. A dwindling corps of Indian riders would keep racing during the next few years, but this day ended Indian national championships, at Harley expense. There had been 44 American racing seasons in which Indian had won premier events; there would be no more.

---

made to ride along these narrow cams. The idea of the four-cammer was to more precisely time the valve movements. Dick Gross had almost turned the inside of Bobby Hill's Sport Scout into a Harley-Davidson, as four cam lobes and ball bearings were all hallmarks of the Milwaukee brand. Gross even used Harley connecting rods!

The Sport Scout built by Art Hafer for Ernie Beckman was ball-bearing outfitted for a while, but Hafer returned to rollers. In the Hafer engine, the pistons were forged, solid-skirt lynite made by the Zollinger Company of Fort Wayne, Indiana, and then lightened for balancing purposes. Later, Hafer used British-made Hepolite pistons. To reduce friction, Hafer left off the third compression ring and ran his motors with two compression rings and one oil ring.

Valves in the Hafer motor were the standard 1-5/8-inch-diameter Sport Scout units. To actuate the valves, Hafer designed his own cam action that incorporated regular Sport Scout cam followers (valve lifters) instead of Bonneville Sport Scout cam followers. The inlet port fed through a duct

that was 1/8 inch larger than stock. The biggest problem experienced was the unreliability of connecting-rod bearings.

Bobby Hill took two 1951 titles, the 25-mile national on the Springfield, Illinois, mile track and the 15-mile national on the Milwaukee, Wisconsin, mile track. As was the custom, Hill was granted the number-one plate for his Springfield victory.

At the 1952 Bay Meadows, California, mile-track race, Bill Tuman and Bobby Hill convincingly demonstrated their horsepower gains since the previous year's Harley-Davidson dominance. Hill was the fastest qualifier at 43.60 seconds. Tuman won the 20-Mile National Championship in 14 minutes and 49.41 seconds, and his 80.95 mile per hour average was a new 20-mile record for mile flat tracks. Bobby Hill again won the Springfield mile, thus holding on to the number-one plate for a second year (over the past four years, Hill had racked up two firsts and two seconds in this most prestigious *continued on page 143*

continued on page 143

Prototype 1952 Warrior. *Indian built about eight prototype road-model Warriors like this one, then decided to delete the road-going twin. The decision was too late to cancel an advertisement for the model in the April 1952 issue of* Cycle. *Owner: Ric Brown.* Jeff Hackett with assistance by *Indian Motorcycle Illustrated*

1951 Warrior. With period saddlebags and windshield closely resembling the original, as well as spotlights, front crashguard, luggage rack, and rear bumper, this example represents the ultimate in 1951 Indian lightweights. Indian vertical twins present a restoration challenge, says Pete Bollenbach, operator of Bollenbach Engineering. That's because many items such as wheel rims and handlebars aren't as yet being remanufactured. Indian Chiefs, on the other hand, can almost be built from scratch with reproduction parts.

1951 Warrior. Indian recognized the mistake of trying to compete against British 500-cc bikes with the 1949 436-cc Scout. For 1950, they introduced the 500-cc Warrior. The larger and now equitable displacement plus the same light weight of 315 pounds (fully serviced), kept the Warrior competitive in unofficial but all-important street warfare. The black tank panel and Indian-head decal were new for 1951. The 1950 tank decal for the road models was similar to that of the 1950 Warrior TT shown elsewhere. This 1951 bike represents the last of the cataloged Warrior road models, as they were mass produced in 1950 and 1951 only. Restoration by Bollenbach Engineering; owner: Joey Bollenbach.

1950-1951 Chief with 1952–1953 cowling. A feature of the 1952 and 1953 Chiefs was the engine cowling, said by Indian advertising to give the Chief the "Vincent look" (the cowling mimicked Vincent's crankcase shape). Expensive, British-built Vincent V-twins were also sold by Indian dealers. This 1950 or 1951 Chief has been customized with the later series' cowling, a popular setup with today's Indian riders. The 1951 and earlier upswept exhaust system has been retained, which is also common on "rider" bikes as contrasted to "show" bikes. Restoration by Starklite Cycle; owner: Bob Stark.

1952–1953 Chief. The 1952–1953 exhaust setup had the pipe running low. Although this had the advantage of allowing large saddlebags to be fitted, oil sling from the chain kept the muffler constantly dirty. This example hasn't been run since cleaned, you can bet on it. The 1952–1953 Chiefs used leftover vertical-twin mufflers—Indian was saving every nickel they could.

Below
1953 Chief. One of the standard colors for 1952 and 1953 was tangerine. When Indian brought out the telescopic fork on the 1950 Chief, it didn't change the frame geometry. To provide for the increased travel of the new front end, they simply allowed the longer fork to raise the steering head about three inches. This resulted in raising the saddle height more than one inch. To regain a low saddle position for 1952, the Wigwam installed smaller 4.75x16-inch tires and a bench-style passenger seat. Restoration by Toney Watson; owner: Dave Leitner.

1953 Chief. British Amal external controls and Amal carburetors were fitted to the 1952 and 1953 Chiefs in order to save money. The Linkert company wasn't interested in an Indian bid for only 500 carburetors per year. Linkert carburetors remained an option on police models. Summing up the 1951 Chief, the June 1951 Cycle, said, "An overall appraisal of the Big Chief's rideability places it in the top bracket. Its rare combination of fore and aft springing (83 percent of weight sprung) plus its seat post suspension and long wheelbase are a boon to any rider's confidence and comfort on highway or byway."

continued from page 139
mile-track race). He finished out Indian's 1952 winnings on the Syracuse, New York, mile track in September, winning the 10-mile championship. Considering there were only three serious Sport Scout campaigners against a dozen or more Harley-Davidson stars, 1952 had been a good Indian year.

Success wasn't as strong in 1953. Hill had several mechanical failures. Bill Tuman won the Springfield mile and kept the number-one plate in the possession of the Indian organization, although like Hill, Tuman would bolt the number-one plate on his overhead-cam Norton single for road races. Bobby Hill won the 10- and 15-mile titles on mile tracks, the latter being his eighth mile-track national championship.

1953, Production Stops

From a December 2, 1953, letter to all dealers:

AN IMPORTANT MESSAGE TO ALL DEALERS: The manage-

1953 Chief. The June 1951 issue of Cycle said, "If you're looking for power, an Indian packs the most of all—80 inches." The 80-ci displacement was achieved by stroking the earlier 74-ci twin from 4-7/16 to 4-13/16 inches; bore remained constant at 3-1/4 inches. The Indian decal shown debuted in 1952 and was suggested by staffer Matt Keevers, editor of Indian News *and the later* Indian *magazine.*

ment of the Indian Company has just completed a study of conditions adversely affecting motorcycle production in the United States. This has led to a decision to suspend assembly of complete motorcycles at Springfield during 1954. The sole purpose of this production holiday is to strengthen the position of the Company for future activities in the motorcycle manufacturing field. During this period, Indian manufacturing facilities will be engaged in parts fabrication and other revenue-producing operations.

An intact and aggressive organization is prepared for action as the United States Distributor for the top-ranking British-built motorcycles. Along with our Indian Brave and Papoose, such famous names as Norton, Vincent, Royal Enfield, A.J.S. and Matchless round out the complete 1954 motorcycle program.

This program, which will be energetically promoted, is realistic and will make money for every participating dealer. We urge your continued loyal support.

Sketchy records and the recollections of an Indian employee, the late Emmett Moore, suggest that only 500 Chiefs were built in each of the last four years, 1950 through 1953. If so, much of the manufacturing was probably done with leftover stock from the days of true mass production of Chiefs that ended with the 1948 models. Canadian enthusiast Don Doody, who made an extensive study of motor numbers, believes 1,300 to 1,500 Chiefs were built in the last two years; this, of course, assumes Indian didn't skip numbers. Regardless, even the heaviest estimate would put Chief production from 1950 through 1953 at a mere token of the pre-1950 levels. In other words, Indian was a long time dying.

The several hundred Indian dealerships were a valuable entity; it was the dealerships more than Indian motorcycles that had gotten Brockhouse interested in an Indian partnership in the first place. Indian dealers carried on in 1954, at first with the same offerings of several British motorcycles that had been available since 1950, then later with only Royal Enfield models. From 1955 through 1959 the Indian shops sold Indian-labeled Royal Enfields with tribal names such as Tomahawk, Trailblazer, Woodsman, and Fire Arrow. Eventually, there was even a Chief model, a 693-cc vertical twin with large-section tires.

The competition scene also wound down slowly. In 1954, Sport Scout-mounted Bill Tuman finished second to Harley-Davidson rider Joe Leonard in the Springfield, Illinois, 25-mile national championship. This was the best post-1953 Indian placing in a national. In August 1957, at St. Paul, Minnesota, Babe DeMay was the last Indian rider to start a national championship from the pole position. An Indian started every Daytona 200 race on the old beach course, the last being in 1960. Max Bubeck kept campaigning his Indian vertical twin, which started life as a standard 26.6-ci (440 cc) Scout. Bubeck won the 1962 Greenhorn 500 on the same machine revamped as a 30.50-ci (500 cc) Warrior and with the addition of Bubeck's home-built, swinging arm rear suspension.

In 1959, the remnants of the once mighty Indian firm passed on to Associated Motorcycles, the British builders of Matchless and AJS. What the British bought was the network of Indian dealerships, which now became "Matchless-Indian" dealers. From 1959 through 1962, these dealers sold Matchless motorcycles that were never labeled "Indian." However, the American-sold Matchless motorcycles did sport Indian names like Apache, Westerner, and Arrow. In 1962, Associated Motorcycles sold their American operation to Joseph Berliner, who, thankfully, laid the Indian name to rest—at least for the time being. Stay tuned.

Postscript

New Zealand's Bert Munro ran his Indian V-twin-powered streamliner at the annual Bonneville, Utah, speed trials from 1962 through 1967. In 1964, Munro and the Indian did 184.00 miles per hour one-way, which was the fastest time of any motorcycle during speed week. His best one-way run of 190.070 miles per hour in 1967 was the all-time fastest speed ever recorded on an Indian and remains so as of this writing. He posted his best two-way average, 183.586 miles per hour, in 1967, which was also his last year to run on the salt. As remarkable as these performances were, they take on extra meaning when you consider that Munro's Indian started life as a 1926 600-cc Scout! Munro designed and made most of the engine internals, even casting his own pistons in New Zealand beach sand! Though a few Indian-mounted hill-climbers stayed in the game, the gutsy, brainy New Zealander was the last to ride an Indian to nationally publicized glory.

The Last Indians

Discussing the photo shown here, Indian staffer Emmett Moore said:

We were in the process of bamboozling the dealers as to the future of Indian plans. We didn't want to admit there weren't to be anymore Indians, and we kept the dealers strung along with stories of production later on. Any time there were machines sitting around like that, Bob [Finn] would go around and take pictures of them to back up our story. I was the official liar. I still got some of the bulletins here. I remember one of them said that due to the fact that the metal used in those machines was classified as strategic, we were unable to get it! Oh, I told all kinds of lies! And there was a day came, when I believe 25 or 30 Indian dealers who'd gotten together descended on the factory en masse, and demanded to know, you know, demanded to see the president of the company, and why there weren't any more motorcycles and so on. That was the end of the lies. We couldn't tell any more lies. That was in 1953.

According to production supervisor Walt Brown, seen in the background in the short-sleeved shirt, these New York City Police Department models are the very last Indians to leave Springfield. This photo was previously unpublished. Companion photos from the same shooting spree were used in the June 1953 issue of *Pow Wow*, the successor to *Indian News*.

Rainbow Chief. *John Polovik invented this "rainbow" paint job in 1942. Indian thought about offering rainbow paint jobs as an extra-cost option, says restorer Bob Stark, but the multi-layer paint scheme required too much time and too much expertise. The Indian script on the tank debuted on the 1947 Chief.*

Indian Today

When the Indian firm announced that production of American-made Indians had ceased, these motorcycles immediately became lemons to the sellers of new motorcycles. Most dealers in American-made Indians went on to other product lines, like the Indian-labeled Royal Enfields or the more popular British brands like Triumph and BSA. Some stayed to the bitter end, finally selling Matchless motorcycles marketed by "The Indian Company."

During its brief lifespan, The Indian Company disposed of all its spare parts for American-made Indians. Gradually, dealers' spare parts for American-made Indians were sold off by most Indian dealers, who were interested only in currently produced motorcycles. The huge stock of Indian parts that had been scattered around the nation in about 500 dealerships became consolidated in a few large inventories. Though some of these inventory builders were practical visionaries, they were also romantics who simply couldn't constrain themselves by thoughts of practicality.

Regardless of their motivations, the early dealers in out-of-production Indians soon reaped their rewards. By 1960, 1953 Chiefs were coveted machines. A few astute rider/owners had seen this coming, and they were happy they had bought one of the last new Chiefs from an Indian shop. In contrast, in 1960 a 1953 Harley-Davidson was just a seven-year-old motorcycle.

Because of its early start, the Indian motorcycle movement now looks back on over 40 years of growth. Consequently, the movement now includes over 40 Indian dealers worldwide. Their services range from repairing a single specific item like the magneto to complete restorations held in stock and waiting for a customer to walk in, buy, and ride out. Every year has seen growth in the stock of reproduced parts and the extent of restoration services. For example, as of this writing, the complex and expensive Indian Four transmission bevel gears are reentering production.

Antique Motorcycle Club of America. *The Antique Motorcycle Club of America (AMCA) was founded in 1954. The first meet drew about two dozen participants with nine motorcycles lined up for judging. That one event was the total calendar for the year. Today, nine national meets are held annually as well as two national road runs, while local chapters conduct their own events. A typical AMCA national meet, this one in Wauseon, Ohio, may display 100 or more old bikes. Indians are always prominent, because they became instant collectibles when Indian ceased production after the 1953 season. Old Harleys didn't catch on for another 20 years.*

Top far left
More Indian fun and games. *The Chief rider in the rear fighting the handlebars is actually on top of the situation. He's winning this slow race, in which the last rider across the line wins. Any rider who puts a foot down is eliminated.*

Top left
Contemporary antique motorcycle racing. *Acting much less than half his age, former Indian dealer Harry Cone lined up to race seriously, then decided to cool it and let the kids fight it out ahead. Competition in the antique motorcycle racing circuit is friendly but tough.*

Customized Four. *Several Fours across the nation have been fitted with the 1950–1953 Indian telescopic fork to improve the ride and modernize appearance. Owner: Billy Doyle.*

Indian motorcycle clubs flourish. Two American Indian clubs, and one Canadian-headquartered club, cater to all models. There is a club for Indian Four enthusiasts, and a club for Series 101 Scout enthusiasts. Field meets, poker runs, local road runs, and long tours, are put together by Indian dealers and Indian clubs. Many Indian owners also belong to the longest-lived old motorcycle club in the United States, the Antique Motorcycle Club of America. The AMCA sponsors dozens of events each year, drawing participants from across the U.S. and around the world. Throughout the world, Indian is strong and on the rise. Britain has two Indian clubs, and Australia has an Indian club. An annual European Indian rally is conducted with the site rotated among nations.

Each publicly displayed Indian is backed up by hundreds of hours of preparation. Often, the exhibited craftsmanship was lovingly carried out by the owner/rider late into the evenings during so-called spare time, and perhaps over a number of years. To many, their hands-on restoration activities range from wrench turning to library research. Restoration is the heart and soul of the movement, and its practitioners find as much joy in reincarnating old iron as they do in riding it. Others, for lack of skill or time turn the work over to professional restoration experts. The pros are expensive, but their work quality makes the proposition a bargain.

Two (count 'em!) Indian Sixes. *After Wichita, Kansas, enthusiast Herb Ottaway built the six-cylinder Indian in the foreground, fellow Wichita antiquer Bud Cox asked Herb's permission to build a duplicate. Go ahead, if you think you can, challenged Herb. Each bike was built from two 1938–1942 engines and one 1940–1942 frame.*

Indian Six. *The crankshafts of each motorcycle were machined from solid iron. Expert welding conceals the interface of the one and one-half Four cases that were combined to build each six-cylinder machine.*

Right
Restoration: The heart of the antique motorcycle movement. *Woody Carson, AMCA board member, is shown working into the night on one of his prized Indians. Time rushes by for "antiquers" when they're so absorbed.* Bob Calkins

Indian watch. *Collecting motorcycle memorabilia is growing more and more popular as the cost of antique bikes themselves pushes beyond the means of more bikers. Indian had batches of items such as this watch made along with such items as cigarette lighters and toys.*

Indian fun and games. *Bob Stark tries his hand at putting a straw in the bottle while riding slowly by—much harder than it may look.*

Club life and nostalgia have spawned the antique motorcycle racing phenomenon. Dozens of races are held annually, falling mainly into two types: dirt track racing and road racing. Nationally advertised race meets are given worldwide publicity, particularly the old-motorcycle races held at Daytona International Speedway each spring. Indians figure prominently in these race meets, winning many of the events for the hand-shift class.

The love for Indian motorcycles is further reflected in the continued strength of the custom movement that has always been part of motorcycling. Although most Indian owners prefer the standard configurations, spice is added to the movement by such time honored customs as the "Chout," a Chief engine in a Scout frame. Other customs that were popular during Indian's production life include civilianized, ex-army Model 841, transverse V-twins and various Indian models outfitted with telescopic front forks, either aftermarket Vard forks of 1946–1949 or Indian forks of 1949-

1953. Rarest of the custom types are the two six-cylinder Indians built by two Wichita, Kansas, tribesmen. The precedent for these was a six-cylinder Henderson put together back in the 1920s. The emphasis on these Indian customs is practicality, hence they are part of a different evolutionary strain than contemporary choppers that emphasize appearance.

So powerful is the Indian name that various attempts have been made over the years to resume production of the American-made classics. These efforts have varied in sincerity and effort, ranging from obvious scams to fruition in the form of prototype machines. In 1968, Floyd Clymer, former publisher of *Cycle* magazine, wasn't contested in his use of the Indian name on several imported two-wheelers, while promising resumption of an updated Sport Scout. The Indian-labeled Clymer imports included at least one Norton, at least one Royal Enfield, 250 hybrids consisting of Velocette engines in Italian frames, and various mopeds and lightweights of both Czech and Italian

Contemporary antique motorcycle racing. *In the Davenport pits we see a Sport Scout fitted with special racing cylinder heads developed by the Indian factory.*

origins. Except for a prototype, the hoped-for Sport Scout never happened.

Following Clymer's death in 1970, his widow sold the so-called trademark rights to the new Indian Motorcycle Company of Gardena, California. This outfit imported minibikes and for a while operated its own factory in Taiwan before going broke in 1976.

From 1978 through 1990, in subplots too complicated to report here, the trademark supposedly passed through the hands of Mr. Carmen DeLeone and his American Moped Associates (another Taiwanese moped business), Derbi Motor Corporation (importer of the Spanish-built Derbi mopeds), back to DeLeone, then a half-interest to Philip S. Zanghi. In 1993, Zanghi ended up in court after being accused of fraud by persons who had invested nearly a million dollars in the Zanghi enterprise. Zanghi, who never produced an Indian motorcycle, had instead licensed clothing manufacturers to use the Indian label on expensive leather jackets.

A New Mexico company, Indian Motorcycle Manufacturing Incorporated, produced a couple of 100-ci (1640 cc) oil-cooled prototypes before financial problems halted the effort in 1994. The New Mexico outfit, led by Wayne Baughman, claimed the Indian trademark was public domain but carefully avoided suits by labeling its prototypes the "Century Chief." As of this writing, Australian businessman Maurits-Hayem Langridge claims he will market an Indian Four in kit form.

Among the recent Indian revivalists, Baughman was unique in two ways. First, he produced two American-made prototypes. Second, Baughman also never claimed to be the legitimate holder of the Indian trademark. The others have made much ado about trademark claims. These claims have been murky at best, each reaching back to the estate of the late Floyd Clymer,

Max Bubeck: Indian sportsman since the 1930s. One of the best things about joining any of the various old-motorcycle clubs throughout the world is the opportunity to meet men who rode 40, 50, and 60 years ago. Here, we see Max Bubeck on the 1915 Indian F-Head he rode from San Diego to New York City. Max started his 1993 transcontinental run on his 76th birthday!

who apparently didn't purchase the trademark from "The Indian Company" of Chicopee Falls, Massachusetts, last known legitimate trademark holder and importer of British-built Matchless motorcycles.

Happily, the original Indian motorcycle lives on, immune from these wheelings and dealings. The eternally young Indians are fittingly represented in the United States and in Europe by carnival thrill riders who still use the beloved 101 Scout. On tiny cylindrical "tracks," Scout riders still thrill fans with barking exhausts and outrageous stunts. No nostalgia here, save to a small minority of onlookers who remember the original "wall of death" shows. Just the proven practicality of 101 Scout handling. You don't need to teach an old dog new tricks, if the old tricks are good enough.

1994 prototype Century Chief V-twin. These were 100 ci (1640 cc) oil-cooled models, featuring three valves per combustion chamber. The Batten-designed 60 degree V-twin used fuel injection. The large pod between the cylinders is the oil tank. The manufacturer, Indian Motorcycle Manufacturing Company of Albuquerque, New Mexico, chose the "Chief" name to avoid trademark difficulties connected with the "Indian" name. Buzz Kanter; Indian Motorcycle Illustrated

Wall of Death rider. *This Series 101 Scout thrill-show rider grabs bills from excited fans at the riding show staged in conjunction with the 1994 Wauseon, Ohio, Antique Motorcycle Club of America national meet. The 101 Scouts are still used here and there in these duties because of their excellent handling. The V-twin sound doesn't hurt a bit either.*

Wall of Death. *Strange as it may seem, the Series 101 Scout is still in use throughout the world as a thrill-show mount. This one has a Harley tank. The old critter hasn't been pampered.*

Appendix
Indian Timeline

1901	January	George Hendee and Oscar Hedstrom sign an agreement to produce motorcycles of Hedstrom's design.
	February	Partners lease tool room of Worcester Bicycle Co. of Middletown, Connecticut, where Hedstrom works on the prototype Indian.
	May	First Indian completed by Hedstrom.
	December	Annual production totals three machines.
1902	July	In its first public competition, Indian wins the first endurance run held in the United States, from Boston, Massachusetts, to New York, New York.
	October	Aurora Mfg. Co. of Aurora, Illinois, agrees to build engines for Indian.
	December	Annual production totals 143 machines.
1903	September	First long-distance track race in the United States won by George Holden at Brighton Beach Track in New York—150 miles and 75 yards in four hours.
	December	Annual production totals 376 machines.
1904	December	Annual production totals 596 machines.
1905	January	Indian is second marque to use twist-grip throttle (Curtiss was first).
	December	Annual production totals 1,181 machines.
1906	September	Transcontinental record of 31-1/2 days, set by Louis J. Mueller of Cleveland, Ohio, and George Holden of Springfield, Massachusetts.
	December	Annual production totals 1,698 machines.
1907	Lineup	First cataloged twins.
	March	Agreement with Aurora terminated; Indian again builds it own engines.
	Summer	T. K. Hastings (American) wins England's 1000-mile trial.
	December	Annual production totals 2,176 machines.
1908	Lineup	Optional magneto ignition.
	December	Annual production totals 3,257 machines.

1909	Lineup	Loop frame.
	May	Enlargement of factory underway, approximately doubling its size and achieving distinctive "wigwam" shape.
	October	Charles Spencer and Charles Gustafson, Jr., set amateur records for 3 through 24 hours and for 200 through 1000 miles at Springfield, Massachusetts, board track.
	December	Annual production totals 4,771 machines.
1910	Lineup	Leaf-spring fork.
	December	Annual production totals 6,137 machines.
1911	Mid-year	First Indian eight-valve twins built.
	July	Transcontinental record. Indian places 1-2-3 in the Isle of Man TT race. Erwin "Cannonball" Baker wins The President's Race.
	August	Jake DeRosier sets official world records for the mile and kilometer at Brooklands track in England.
	December	At year's end, Indian holds all 121 American speed and endurance records.
	The Year	Annual production totals 9,763 machines.
1912	June	Charles B. Franklin sets world records for 2, 4, 5, and 6 hours and becomes the first rider to travel 300 miles in less than 300 minutes, at the Brooklands track in England.
	September	Worst motorcycle racing accident occurs at Newark, New Jersey, motordrome when two riders and six spectators are killed. This accident marked the beginning of the end for this type of racing, which had been dominated by Indian.
	December	Annual production totals 19,500 machines.
1913	Lineup	Cradle spring frame.
	March	Oscar Hedstrom retires. Indian's most famous racer, Jake DeRosier, is buried in Springfield after nearly a year of treatment following a racing accident.
	October	Company incorporates.
	December	Annual production of 32,000 motorcycles and profit of $1.3 million were both all-time highs. The first drive-in gasoline station opened in Pittsburgh, Pennsylvania.

1914	Lineup	Hendee Special with electric starter.
	May	Cannonball Baker sets transcontinental record of 11 days, 12 hours, and 10 minutes.
	July	Glenn "Slivers" Boyd wins inaugural Dodge City 300—only win for Indian in this premier event.
	December	Annual production totals 25,000 motorcycles. Annual profit of $712,000.
	The Year	The first traffic light was used in Cleveland, Ohio.
1915	Lineup	First generator-equipped models.
	December	Annual production totals 21,000 motorcycles and 3,200 sidecars. Annual profit of $422,000.
1916	Lineup	First Powerplus side-valve motors.
	July	President George Hendee retires.
	December	Annual production totals 22,000 motorcycles and 3,700 sidecars. Annual profit is $206,000.
1917	Lineup	Black hubs, spokes, and rims on all models.
	December	Annual production totals 20,500 motorcycles and 5,600 sidecars. Annual profit of $540,000.
1918	December	Annual production totals 22,000 motorcycles and 13,300 sidecars. Annual profit of $733,000.
1919	December	Annual production totals 21,500 motorcycles. Annual profit of $937,000.
1920	Lineup	First Scouts.
	January	Official beginning of Scout series with unit powerplant.
	April	Gene Walker sets a series of world records at Daytona Beach. These marks were the last officially sanctioned maximum-speed world records for an American-made motorcycle.
	April	Albert "Shrimp" Burns becomes first rider to win a national championship at a 100-plus–mile-per-hour pace on a "stock" machine, a Powerplus racer, at Beverly Hills, California (15-mile race).
	August	In Australia, H. A. Parsons sets a 24-hour record of 1,114-1/2 miles.
	November	Herbert "Bert" LeVack sets kilometer and mile records for England (Brooklands) at 95.2 miles per hour.
	The Year	Indian won 14 national championship races at distances of 1 through 50 miles, with total winning mileage of 200 miles, but Harley-Davidson won 511 miles of racing spread over only three races.
1921	April	Gene Walker sets 11 official world's records including 115.79 miles per hour over a one kilometer distance.
	June	Indian wins team award at Isle of Man TT races.
	July	Herbert "Bert" LeVack wins 500-mile race at Brooklands, the longest motorcycle race ever conducted there. Indian loses its fourth consecutive Dodge City 300.
1922	Lineup	First Chiefs, 61 ci.
1923	Lineup	First 74-ci Chiefs.
	May	Paul Remaley sets Three-Flag record of 46 hours and 58 minutes on a Scout.
	June	Last Indian team entry at Isle of Man.
	July	Remaley repeats his Three-Flag record, beating a Henderson time.
	August	Freddie Dixon wins Belgian Gran Prix on a Powerplus "half-twin."
	The Year	Remaley sets transcontinental record on Scout, 5 days, 17 hours, and 10 minutes.
1924	Lineup	New pull-action fork. Last year of the Standard (formerly, the Powerplus).
1925	Lineup	Prince 350-cc single. Removable heads on Scout and Prince.
	October	Paul Anderson sets French record of 135.71 miles per hour, with fastest one-way run of 159.08 miles per hour, at Arpajon Speedway; record not recognized by F.I.C.M. due to alleged timing-equipment irregularities.
	The Year	London Branch closed. East Springfield equipment and machinery sold.
1926	January	Johnny Seymoure sets American 30.50-ci and 61-ci records at Daytona Beach.
	September	M. L. "Curly" Fredericks sets all-time maximum average speed for board tracks, of 120.3 miles per hour at Salem, New Hampshire.
1927	Lineup	Indian Ace introduced. Full range includes singles, twins, and fours. First 45-ci Scouts. Removable heads on Chief.
1928	Lineup	First Indian Fours. Second and last year of full-range lineup. 101 Scouts introduced in Spring.
	The Year	Indian won all national championship races due to Harley-Davidson's new no-racing policy.
1929	The Year	Indian purchases Hartford Outboard Motor Company.
1930	April	Indian common stock valued at $11.75.
	May	E. Paul du Pont elected president of Indian. Outboard-motor business offered for sale.

	December	Management considers selling half of the Wigwam to The Tasty Yeast Company.
1931	Lineup	Last year of 101 Scouts.
	The Year	Factory piece-work rate cut 15 percent; other hourly workers' wages cut 12 percent; salaried employees work Saturday mornings without extra pay and have wages cut 21 percent.
		Annual production totals 4,557 machines (Harley-Davidson built 10,500).
1932	Lineup	The "New Look" models with taller frames and longer forks.
		First 30.50-ci Scout Ponies. First Scouts with Chief frames.
	January	Factory piece-work rate cut 10 percent; other hourly workers' wages cut 10 percent. Layoffs: Tool Room, 30; Engineering, 4; Order, 3. Consideration given to providing Sears Roebuck a revamped Prince without front wheel brake or any accessories.
	February	Plans underway to combine the Purchasing and Control departments to save three salaries; curtail advertising, including *Indian News;* and curtail Engineering department activities.
		Production rate increased from 15 to 20 motorcycles per day. Japanese order for 35 motorcycles (mostly military) received.
	March	Layoffs: Engineering, 2; Racing, 1 (Gustafson); Purchasing/Control, 3; Security 1 (gate closed); Sales, 5 or 6. Elevator servicing moved under Service Department and only one elevator to be used.
	May	Factory goes on four-day week.
	November	du Pont offers for sale his controlling interest in DuPont Motors Inc.
	December	Management decides not to take on an air-conditioner line.
	The Year	Annual production totals 2,360 machines (Harley-Davison sold 6,841).
1933	Lineup	First dry sump lubrication.
	February	Accounting department notifies general manager that the company will not be able to meet its next payroll; manager obtains $10,000 loan to meet payroll. Office force put on 2/3 time. Factory closed for one week (without pay to employees). Financial planning includes consideration of bankruptcy. DuPont Motors declares bankruptcy.
	August	General Manager meets with employee representatives, decides to raise wages 15 percent in line with recent area wage increases, addresses all factory employees, and encourages formation of an employ-

		ees' association (as opposed to a union).
	The Year	Annual production totals 1,667 machines, the all-time lowest in the Wigwam. (Harley-Davidson built/sold 3,703, also its all-time lowest since its pioneer years.)
1934	Lineup	First Sport Scouts.
	The Year	Annual production totals 2,809 machines. (Harley-Davidson built between 9,000 and 10,000 for the comparable 12-month period, prior to extending their 1934-sales-season by 6 months.)
1935	Lineup	Three tank-panel styles offered, except on Scout Pony. Optional four-speed transmission on Chief and Sport Scout.
	December	Indian common stock valued at $2.50.
	The Year	Annual production totals 3,715 machines (Harley-Davidson built approximately 11,000).
1936	Lineup	Scout renamed "Standard Scout."
		First "upside-down" Fours. Chiefs, Sport Scouts, and Standard Scouts use "T" oil lines for upper-end lubrication.
	The Year	Annual production totals 5,028 machines (Harley-Davidson built approximately 11,000).
1937	Lineup	Last "upside-down" Fours. Last year of "T" lines on Chiefs, Sport Scouts, and Scouts. Scout Pony renamed "Junior Scout."
	January	Ed Kretz wins inaugural Daytona 200. Harley-Davidson sets American (unrestricted, Class A) record at Daytona Beach, ending Indian's reign as fastest American motorcycle since 1926.
	The Year	Annual production totals 6,030 machines (Harley-Davidson built 12,100).
1938	Lineup	Tank-mounted instrument panels, except on Junior Scout. New four-cylinder engine.
	March	Roland "Rollie" Free sets Class C 45-ci and 74-ci records at Daytona Beach.
	September	Fred Ludlow sets Class C 45-ci and 74-ci records at Bonneville.
	The Year	Annual production totals 3,650 machines. (Harley-Davidson built 7,658 motorcycles, 519 Servi-Cars, 896 sidecars, 74 package trucks, 298 chassis, and 489 radios. Harley President Walter Davidson used the figure 8,177 in his report to stockholders, that number being the total of motorcycles and Servi-Cars.)
1939	The Year	Annual production totals 3,012 machines (eight months). (Harley-Davidson built 7,695 motorcycles, 660 Servi-Cars, 1,339 sidecars, 122 Package Trucks, and 160 chassis—these are 12-month totals.)

1940	Lineup	Skirted fenders on all models. Spring frame on Fours and Chiefs. Junior Scout renamed "Thirty-Fifty."
	February	General Manager Loren "Joe" Hosley dies.
	The Year	Annual production totals 10,431 machines including 5,000 Chiefs built for the French army (Harley-Davidson sold 10,855 units, almost all civilian models).
1941	Lineup	Spring frame on Sport Scout.
	The Year	Annual production totals 8,739 machines (Harley-Davidson built 18,428 units).
1931–1941		Total Indian production during these du Pont years was 43,259. Total Harley-Davidson production for the same years was 110,459.
1942	Lineup	No 1942 sales catalogs printed. Token production of 1942 civilian models did not include Thirty-Fifties (formerly called Junior Scouts and Scout Ponies). Chrome trim not used on later-built machines. Fours not offered on West Coast, except for police orders.
	The Year	Annual production totals 16,647 machines (Harley-Davidson built 29,603). Indian takes over the Atlanta and New York dealerships.
1943	The Year	Annual production totals 16,456 machines (Harley-Davidson sold 29,243).
1944	June	War Production Board authorizes production of 1,700 Model 345 motorcycles for essential police and civilian use.
	The Year	Annual production totals 3,881 machines (Harley-Davidson built 17,006).
1945	March	Roland Burnstan elected president; E. Paul du Pont elected chairman of the board.
	August	Work week cut from 60 to 48 hours.
	November	Ralph B. Rogers elected president.
	The Year	Annual production totals 2,070 machines (Harley-Davidson built over 10,000).
1942–1945		Total Indian production in the war years was 39,054. Total Harley-Davidson production during the same years was over 88,000.
1946	Lineup	Chief is the only model offered; has new girder fork.
	February	Plans underway to move Torque Manufacturing Company and Ideal Power Lawn Mower Company to the Indian plant.
	The Year	Annual production totals 3,621 machines (Harley-Davidson built 15,554, although the plant was on strike for six weeks). However, a total of 6,974 1946-model Chiefs were built; the difference is that 1946 models were also sold from September through December 1946, four months which were part of Fiscal Year 1947.
1947	February	Indian reorganizes; Atlas Corporation, Chemical Bank, and Marine Midland Bank provide financing. Johnny Spiegelhoff wins Daytona 200 on under-the-table, prewar, big-base Sport Scout.
	April	Indian announces that the Wigwam is for sale.
	May	Max Bubeck wins Greenhorn Enduro in southern California on a 1939 Four.
	August	R. B. Rogers Companies merged with Indian. Ideal Lawn Mower Company and Torque Manufacturing Company merge with Indian.
	The Year	Annual production totals 11,849 (Harley-Davidson built 20,000).
1948	March	G. Briggs Weaver honored by West Coast dealers for his development of the new lightweight models. Floyd Emde wins Daytona 200 on 648 Scout.
	June	Max Bubeck rides Chase/Bubeck "Chout" to 135.58 miles per hour at Rosamond Dry Lake, California, the highest speed ever attained on an unstreamlined Indian to this day.
	July	First vertical-twin Scouts and Arrow singles offered for sale.
	August	Official opening of new plant in East Springfield, Massachusetts.
	September	*Business Week* publishes article about Indian's postwar program.
	November	250 employees laid off; 800 left on payroll.
1949	Lineup	First production Scout 26-ci (440 cc) vertical twins and Arrow 13-ci (220 cc) singles. No Chiefs offered.
	June	Indian protests Springfield's award of police motorcycle contract to Harley-Davidson.
1946–1949		Total Indian production during the Rogers era was approximately 24,500 motorcycles, of which approximately 18,500 were Chiefs and 6,000 were lightweight models. Total Harley-Davidson production during these same years was 90,457.
1950	Lineup	Chiefs reintroduced with telescopic forks. First Warrior 30.50-ci (500 cc) twins. First Warrior TT twins. Last 26-ci Scouts and 13-ci Arrows sold (assembled from leftover stock).

	January	Ralph Rogers resigns.
	September	E. Paul du Pont dies.
1951	Lineup	Arrow replaced by British-built Brave.
	August	Bobby Hill wins Springfield, Illinois, 25-mile national, giving him the No. 1 plate for the 1952 season.
1952	Lineup	Last year for Warrior and Warrior TT.
	August	Bobby Hill wins Springfield 25-mile national again, giving him the No. 1 plate for the 1953 season.
1953	Lineup	Last year of American-made Indians. Production of approximately 500 machines, largely from leftover stocks.
	May	The last American-made Indians are assembled in the Myrick Building of downtown Springfield.
	August	Bill Tuman wins the Springfield 25-miler, giving him the No. 1 plate for the 1954 season.
	October	At Williams Grove, Pennsylvania, Ernie Beckman wins the 8-mile national (half-mile track), the last national championship race won on an Indian.
1954	Lineup	Indian dealers offer only Royal Enfields (without the Indian label).
	July	Massachusetts State Police orders Harley-Davidsons, ending a 33-year run of Indian use.
1955	Lineup	Indian dealers sell Indian-labeled Royal Enfields.
1957	August	At St. Paul, Minnesota, Babe DeMay is the last Indian rider to start a national championship from the pole position.
1962	The Year	Max Bubeck wins California's Greenhorn Enduro on modified Indian vertical twin. Bert Munroe sets class record at Bonneville speed trials of 162.149 miles per hour on a 51-ci (850 cc), overhead-valve twin built up from a Scout base.
	July	"The Indian Company" of Chicopee Falls, Massachusetts, announces its liquidation.
1966	The Year	Munroe ups Bonneville class record to 168.066 miles per hour on 56-ci (920 cc) overhead-valve Scout derivative.
1967	The Year	Munroe sets new class record of 183.586 miles per hour on 58-ci (950 cc) overhead-valve Scout derivative. One-way run of 190.070 miles per hour was the all-time fastest speed achieved on an Indian.
1973	The Year	Larry Smith wins the Goshen, Indiana, hillclimb, the last national championship hillclimb won on an Indian.

Comparison of Indian and Harley-Davidson Production

1931-1949

Year	Indian	Harley-Davidson
1931	4,557	10,500
1932	2,360	6,841
1933	1,667	3,703
1934	2,809	9,500 (approx. 16-month season)
1935	3,715	11,000 (approx.)
1936	5,028	11,000 (approx.)
1937	6,030	12,100
1938	3,650	8,177
1939	3,012	8,355
1940	10,431	10,855
1941	8,739	18,428
1942	16,647	29,603
1943	16,456	29,243
1944	3,881	17,006
1945	2,070	10,000+ (approx.)
1946	3,621	15,554
1947	11,849	20,000
1948–1949	9,000 (approx.)	54,903

Index